the detox

handbook

maria costantino

the detox

handbook

maria costantino

Published by SILVERDALE BOOKS
An imprint of Bookmart Ltd
Registered number 2372865
Trading as Bookmart Ltd
Desford Road
Enderby
Leicester LE19 4AD

D&S Books Ltd
Kerswell,
Parkham Ash, Bideford
Devon, England
EX39 5PR

e-mail us at:-
enquiries@dsbooks.fsnet.co.uk

This edition printed 2004

ISBN 1-856057-18-6

Creative Director: Sarah King
Editor: Sarah Harris
Project editor: Sally MacEachern
Designer: Axis Design
Photography: Colin Bowling

Printed in China

3 5 7 9 1 0 8 6 4

contents

chapter 1

what is detox?

what is detox?

Pick up a copy of any of today's magazines and you'll find at least one

article dedicated to health, beauty or diet. All too often we look for – and

are offered – short-term, 'quick fix' solutions: marvellous potions and

lotions in beautiful packages that the travelling snake oil salesman of the

19th century could only have dreamed of! There is no doubt though that

psychologically, the mere acts of buying one of these products,

unwrapping it, and dipping our fingers in for the very first time, do give us

pleasure: it makes us feel better. But all too often this feeling of wellbeing

is short lived.

We really do know that the key to feeling good and looking great is that thing called 'diet'. For far too long the word 'diet' has been synonymous with weight loss and, consequently, we have punished our bodies for 'its failures' with harsh, restrictive 'regimes' that have left our bodies exhausted and spirits broken. It's time to start thinking about the word 'diet' in its truest sense: it comes from the Greek word *diata* which means 'way of living'. Diet does not mean a set of calorie counted recipes designed by one person for millions of others to endure. While all our bodies 'work' – in a mechanical sense – in the same ways, in truth, everyone's body 'functions' slightly differently.

diet is too often associated with weight loss.

'Diet' means your way of living: what clothes or colours suit you and make you feel good or are special to you, the type of movements your body makes and enjoys, and the way in which you 'wind up' for a busy day and 'wind down' at the end of it. It is also about the foods or drinks you put in your body because what you eat is going to have a significant impact on the way you feel, how you look, how energised and 'vital' you feel, and in the long term, how healthy your body – and spirit – will be.

The human body is a marvellous machine with its own inbuilt mechanisms to keep it 'ticking over'. But like any 'machine' bodies can break down. To keep it running smoothly it must have the right 'fuel' and it must be routinely and regularly serviced. We probably spend more time and energy making sure our cars are in good condition than we do our own bodies! We check for rust, dents, and scratches on our car bodies, listen for squeaks and knocks from the engine and even talk sweetly and encouragingly to it! But when it comes to our bodies, we'll put up with feeling sick until we break down completely, then treat the symptoms and forget all about what caused the breakdown in the first place!

the way we live places additional stress on our bodies.

The way we live today means that we are also putting a lot of additional stresses and strains on our bodies: noise, lack of sleep, inappropriate food, alcohol and cigarettes, often combined with a lack of exercise, mean that our bodies have to cope with the human equivalent every day of a stock car race! Consequently more and more people are finding that they are not only 'breaking down' more frequently, they aren't recovering fully after each breakdown. This is because their bodies have not been able to deal with and eliminate the toxins that have built up. Detoxing is a way of eliminating these toxins – it's a bit like an oil change on your car – allowing your body to recover its strength and vitality and let the energy flow!

Detoxing is not a new 'fad': it's been around for thousands of years. The ancient Egyptians detoxed: Cleopatra famously bathed in milk to slough off old skin, encourage new soft skin and keep her complexion beautifully fresh. Shen Nung, the Chinese emperor who died in 2698 B.C., kindly used himself as a human guinea pig to discover which plants were poisonous and then compiled the *Canon of Herbs* containing 252 plant descriptions and notes on their effects – good and bad – on the human body.

The ancient Greeks advised garlic as a purifier of the blood while the mathematician and philosopher Pythagorus (571–496 B.C.) condemned eating beans because they produced 'foul humours'!

garlic has been recommended as a healthy food since the time of the ancient Greeks.

In the 13th century in Christian Europe, all healthy adults were forbidden by the church to eat meat on three days a week. By the 15th century Fridays were obligatory fasting days and annual fasts, such as Rogation Days, Advent, and Lent – which lasted then as now, six weeks – meant that as well as meat, eggs and dairy foods were also banned. Fasting was not viewed as simply 'spiritually' beneficial – and a way of demonstrating publicly one's religious devotion – by this time, knowledge about the 'nature' of foods and their effects on the human body was widespread. John Russell, who was Marshal to the Duke of Gloucester in the 1440s, wrote an instruction manual, *The Babees Book*, in verse form. This book was designed to help train young men of noble birth become the servants of princes. Not only does Russell instruct them on medieval courtesies and how to carve at a banquet, but he also includes advice about nutrition, and wrote that milk, cream and curds 'close a man's stomach and so are binding'. Another 15th-century text called *A Leechbook* consists of no fewer than 1074

'medicinal cookery' recipes – many of which are purgatives to 'void wind' and deal with what seemed to be a common medieval dietary problem – constipation! Today we would use the polite phrase 'feeling bloated', but it remains one of the signs that our bodies are having trouble dealing with some of the foods we eat, and in eliminating accumulated waste and toxins.

Detoxing is not about denying your body its 'fuel'. On the contrary, detoxing is about listening to your body – like you do to your car – and making sure it has the right fuel for optimum performance! Certain types of foods actually decrease our energy levels and make our minds dull and the same foods can be difficult for the body to deal with so they build up and put extra strain on the body's digestive system. The result is that as our body becomes over burdened, we start to suffer minor complaints – indigestion, flatulence and constipation, as well as headaches, poor skin, hair and nails, and even mild depression.

Even the 15th-century author of *The Leechbook* had a pretty good idea about the effects of some foods when he wrote:

'All bitter things comfort the stomach.

All sweet things enfeeble it.

Roasted things are dry.

All raw things annoy the stomach.

Whoso will keep continual health, [must] keep his stomach so that he put not too much therein when he hath appetite, nor take anything into it when he hath no need.

And then continual health will ensue.'

a Leechbook or Collection of Medical Recipes of the Fifteenth Century: MS136 of the Literary Society of London. Transcribed and edited by Warren R. Dawson, Macmillan and Co. Ltd 1934.

With all the advances that modern life has brought us – education, technology, medicine, and better nutrition from an enormous variety of foodstuffs both fresh and preserved to conserve their goodness, to name just a few – you would think that we would be the healthiest people alive, full of vigour and vitality, living our lives to the full and remaining fit and healthy into very advanced old age. In fact the opposite is more true: instead of using the knowledge available to improve ourselves, our busy, outwardly focussed, modern lives do little to promote a healthy life and all too often we are willing to accept that poor health in all its manifestations is just a 'fact of life'.

with all the nutritious foods available, we SHOULD be able to live a long and healthy life.

What detoxing does is help us to take the time to focus a little more on ourselves: to listen to what our bodies are trying to tell us. Now, instead of ignoring symptoms – or by suppressing them with the myriad of 'over-the-counter' medicines freely available – we can recognise and interpret those 'bodily messages' and take steps to change our diet – our way of living – for the better so those symptoms don't reoccur.

One of the best things about our modern lives is the availability of information and knowledge – from the past and from the present – and from a wide variety of different cultural experiences. Detoxing draws on a wide range of sources including traditional Chinese medicine, yoga, tai chi and qi gong, reflexology and massage, aromatherapy, Bach Flower remedies, hydro (water based) therapies (such as saunas, thalassotherapy)

detoxing enables us to listen to our bodies and to change our diets for the better.

and a whole host of other approaches to healing and improving our bodies, minds and spirits. For a long time, many of these therapies were the preserve of the lucky few initiated into the knowledge or those rich enough to be able to afford expensive 'treatments'. Detoxing allows each of us to explore and experience the range of therapies and to find the ones most suited to our own bodies and lifestyles.

with all the complementary therapies available, it is easier for us to improve our health and wellbeing.

why detox?

Detoxing is about restoring the body's balance. The body's system and its internal organs do a pretty good – and often thankless – job of processing food, fuelling the body and eliminating waste. But when we put extra strain on our bodies, we can upset the balance and things can start to go wrong. We may not necessarily feel 'ill' but there may be warning signs that all is not well: tiredness and lethargy – both physical and emotional – irregular bowel movements, spots, pimples, blemishes and a generally poor complexion, mouth ulcers and chapped lips, itching or sore eyes, dull hair, weak nails, headaches, menstrual cramps and heavy flow. In short, anything that 'gets you down' is a sign that something is wrong, that our body is 'out of balance'.

We can often see these side effects and warning signs immediately after we have 'over indulged' – we've eaten and drunk too much – and of the wrong things like alcohol, coffee or tea; smoked cigarettes; missed meals and instead snacked on fast food; stayed up late too often and deprived ourselves of sleep for too long. The horrible truth is that this is how we live our lives every day, so it's no wonder we feel so bad! It's time to make some changes, to take back the control of our minds, bodies and spirits, to make a 'clean sweep'!

headaches or generally feeling down are warning signs that something is wrong.

our livers have to deal
with all the toxins we
put into our bodies.

The liver, kidneys, lymphatic system and our skin are all organs crucial to the smooth effective running of our bodies. The liver takes out any poisonous or toxic substances that enter our bodies – via the foods we eat and from the environment. The liver converts these substances into a form that the body can utilise immediately or store for future use. What isn't required is eliminated. Our kidneys work to maintain the correct level of fluid in the body, making sure that vital minerals such as potassium and sodium are regulated. The kidneys also act as a filter, removing toxic wastes from the blood and eliminating them from the body in the form of urine. The lymphatic system is also part of the body's natural waste disposal unit: in various parts of the body, glands produce a liquid called lymph which absorbs dead cells, waste products from food and excess fluids in the body and takes them to lymph nodes.

So that nothing of value is eliminated, the lymph nodes filter the waste in the lymph once more and pass it onto the blood which is circulated to the liver, kidneys or skin, where it is passed out of the body in the forms of perspiration, urine or faeces.

Our skin is in fact the largest organ in our body and its functions are varied. Not only does it form a physical barrier to protect our internal organs, it is semi-permeable, and thus regulates what can enter and leave the body – for example it helps us to prevent excess water loss that can lead to dehydration. Our skin also produces an acidic secretion that kills off any micro organisms which may have landed on us! It also maintains our body temperature – when we get hot, we sweat, which cools the skin and body as it evaporates from the surface of the skin, while when we get cold, the body sends signals to dilate the blood vessels to reduce the flow of blood to the top layers of the skin in order to reduce heat loss. Most importantly, because our skin is visible, it acts as a mirror to what is going on inside our bodies: our skin is our best early warning system, guarding against danger and reacting to indicate a problem.

the health of our skin is a good indicator of how our bodies are working.

Detoxing is a highly effective way of keeping all these vital eliminating organs in balance and in tip top condition, but more importantly, being aware of how we can decrease the number of toxins which we introduce into our bodies will mean that there is less stress on the body's natural system.

so many of today's foodstuffs are highly processed, with hardly any of their natural goodness.

Many of the foodstuffs we eat on a daily basis need closer consideration: the food production and processing industries over the last 50 years or so have used an increasing number of additives and preservatives, along with foodstuffs which are now highly refined – often to the point where the 'natural goodness' has all but been removed and has to be replaced with chemically synthesised vitamins. Most of the time, our bodies cannot assimilate these foods and if they are not eliminated, they can become toxins in the body. Consequently, our bodies are so busy dealing with all the accumulated toxins that it cannot deal with new foodstuffs put into our system and so much of it is only partially digested before it is added to the 'waste', perpetuating the cycle.

Most times, when we take steps towards 'making a clean sweep' we get depressed about the way we feel and look: we might feel tired, seem to have a short temper, and get fed up with the state of our hair and skin. It's not surprising we feel this way: it's a bit like a drug addict going 'cold turkey'! Our bodies have become 'addicted' to a complex diet of highly refined, highly processed foods full of chemicals, and it's really having to struggle to 'get clean' – to get back its natural balance. What we tend to do when we try to 'get healthy' is cut out all the things we know to be bad for us, but what we fail to do is to give ourselves the things that our poor mistreated bodies really need. Detoxing gives us a way of avoiding the causes of the toxins in our bodies, while providing us with replacements in the form of specific, unprocessed, pure foods needed to fuel our bodies and help it regain its natural balance.

we need to not only eliminate what is bad for us, but also ensure we eat enough of what is good for us.

elements of (

Detoxing consists of four elements: foods and juices; cleansing

substances and regimes; gentle exercises, and 'lifestyle' projects. You

can, however, personalise your detox programme to suit your own

individual needs: you can completely cleanse your system over a period

of weeks – one of the best ways of integrating a new healthy lifestyle

without giving your body too much of a shock; you can do a quick-fix

detox for dealing with those times when you over-indulged the night

before; or you can treat yourself to a weekend detox – 48 hours of sheer

indulgence looking after 'number one'.

etox

It's not enough however just to have a healthy body: man – and woman – cannot live by bread alone, even if it is whole grain! Thinking straight and thinking positively about yourself helps to develop confidence and self-esteem, so a 'mind detox' also helps. If we don't value ourselves, how on earth can we value anyone else? If we're tired, grumpy, bloated and blue, then our relationships with friends, colleagues, family and lovers will also suffer. It may be time to detox our relationships – letting go of the past perhaps, or allowing in the new. You can also detox your home: clear out the clutter, get rid of the old, out of date, or no longer used items in your cupboards, drawers and wardrobe!

being physically healthy is only part of the detox 'trick' – if you are miserable or suffer from low self-esteem, you won't feel the full detox benefit.

getting started

Detoxing is very gentle. You don't have to make great concessions in

your everyday life, and, what's more, because you'll look and feel better,

you'll enjoy your life even more. The hardest thing about detoxing is

deciding to do it! If you really do want to make changes in your life –

changes for the better – then break the cycle and start now

Before you begin to detox, make sure you read this book all the way through first! Not only will you find out what you need – and need to avoid – but you'll find information on exercises, recipes, body treatments and maintaining your system when you've detoxed. By reading through the book first, you will be able to make adjustments to suit your own body, mind and life – to personalise your own detox programme.

start making changes in your life now!

There are however a few reasons why
you should not detox. You
should not start
detoxing if   pregnant
you are:

breast-feeding

currently undergoing any medical treatment
for any illness or condition, or are
recovering from a serious illness

taking prescribed or non-prescribed drugs

already on a medically advised and supervised diet

seriously underweight

suffering from an eating disorder

suffering from any
psychological complaint   If you have any doubts
whatsoever about your health,
always consult a qualified medical
practitioner for advice.

It's the condition of your body now, at this moment – and that of your spirit and even home surroundings – which determines how and when you start to detox. It's a good idea to take a look at your diary: look for when you can devote time to you. If you can't do this straight away, don't worry, you can use any spare moments to get ready. There will be some things you need to get, so you can shop for these and have them ready for when you start. You'll find a 'shopping list' later on, but don't be alarmed: you'll probably find that you already have many of the items.

try and take the time to prepare to detox. Make space for yourself so you don't feel pressured.

If you are a junk food junkie, a drinker, a smoker, or someone who needs the kick of caffeine to help you start the day, then you realise that there are some pretty important decisions that need to be made. Be completely honest and circle or tick the answer that best describes your current state of health and wellbeing.

questionnaire

How good is your current diet – your way of life?

Very healthy	(3 points)
Pretty healthy	(2 points)
Unhealthy	(1 point)
In self-destruct mode	(0 points)

How active are you?

I have an active job/life with plenty of regular exercise	(3 points)
I have a sedentary job but do some exercise	(2 points)
I have a sedentary job and take no exercise	(1 point)
I have trouble walking to the bus stop	(0 points)

How would you rate your energy levels?

Good	(3 points)
OK	(2 points)
Low	(1 point)
Asleep	(0 points)

How much water do you drink per day?

1.5 l (3 pints)	(3 points)
3–4 glasses	(2 points)
Fewer than 3 glasses	(1 point)
An ice cube in a gin and tonic	(0 points)

How much coffee, tea or canned drinks such as cola do you drink per day?

Few or none	(3 points)
3–4 cups	(2 points)
5–6 cups	(1 point)
A gallon	(0 points)

How much fresh fruit or vegetables do you eat every day?

4–5 portions	(3 points)
2–3 portions	(2 points)
1–2 portions	(1 point)
Chips	(0 points)

How many units of alcohol do you drink per week?

1–4 units	(3 points)
4–6 units	(2 points)
8–12 units	(1 point)
You can't remember	(0 points)

How many cigarettes do you smoke a day?

None	(3 points)
Someone else's because they offered	(0 points)
1 or 2 just to be social	(0 points)
5	(0 points)
10	(0 points)
20	(0 points)
Like a chimney	(0 points)

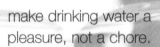

How did you do? If you scored 14 points or more, then you can start detoxing without too much trouble.

If you scored fewer than 14 points, then before you start detoxing, you need to make a few changes to your lifestyle. So, before you begin to detox:

1 take a little exercise: Don't go mad and start running a marathon – your body just won't take it! Instead, try a short walk at lunchtime; use the stairs rather than the elevator or escalator; or walk a little of the way home – get off at the bus stop before your usual one and walk the rest of the way.

make drinking water a pleasure, not a chore.

2 increase your water intake: You should be drinking at least 1 litre (2 pints) of water per day. Replace those cans of cola or cups of coffee or tea with some cool mineral water. Make drinking water a pleasure: don't drink straight from a bottle, use an attractive glass instead and add a slice of lemon or lime.

3 reduce your alcohol intake: cut back to half your normal weekly intake and try to avoid 'over indulging' at weekends.

make small changes in your life to start with – like walking to work instead of driving – you will soon notice the benefits.

4 reduce your caffeine intake: like alcohol and nicotine, caffeine is an addictive and it's hard to go 'cold turkey'! Start by reducing the amount of tea or coffee you drink by half: buy yourself a new teacup and saucer or a new coffee cup – one that's not quite as big as the one you are currently using! Buy the smaller-sized, take-away cup and ease off from the double espressos. Whether it's home brewed or from a store, don't drink on the run. Sit down, relax and drink the cup slowly. That way you'll enjoy it more and need less through the day.

eat more fruit and vegetables.

5 increase your intake of fresh fruit and vegetables: ideally you should be eating three portions of fruit and three portions of vegetables each day. A portion of fruit is an apple or a pear, while a portion of vegetables is just one large spoonful. Thanks to air freight, it is possible to eat tropical or exotic produce all year round.

6 quit smoking: No excuses, just do it!

cut back on caffeine – try and break the habit slowly.

food intoleranc

If you ticked lots of '3 point' answers in the questionnaire, you would

expect to feel good and look great. But, if in spite of all your efforts you

are still feeling 'under the weather', and you can't work out why you feel

this way, then it may be because you have a food intolerance. Food

intolerances are relatively common today, the problem is, that we just

don't realise we have one.

Because of the huge variety of foods and drinks available to us in our daily lives, it is often hard to identify which foodstuffs our bodies are finding difficult to process. A food intolerance is not the same as being allergic to something. Someone who has an allergy – to nuts for example – will, after eating one, develop acute and immediate symptoms that can be life threatening. Food intolerances, on the other hand, provoke delayed reactions, which while they are not life threatening, do interfere with the body's overall wellbeing. By avoiding the foodstuffs we know or suspect to be the major culprits, we can give our bodies time to 'recover' and rebalance.

there are several foods which can be found to cause an intolerance.

Do you have an intolerance? To help you find out, look at the statements below and circle yes or no if the statement is true of you:

i suffer from flatulence (wind) and/or indigestion a lot   yes/no

i feel bloated a lot of the time   yes/no

i get constipation and/or diarrhoea frequently   yes/no

my weight fluctuates up and down for no obvious reason   yes/no

i don't lose weight even when I count calories   yes/no

i get fluid retention: my feet and hands are often swollen   yes/no

i want to sleep after eating   yes/no

i feel tired even after a good long sleep at night   yes/no i have peaks and troughs of energy through the day   yes/no

i get headaches/migraines frequently   yes/no

my joints are stiff and my muscles often ache   yes/no

i have spots/acne/skin complaints   yes/no

i have dandruff   yes/no

i crave certain foods   yes/no

i always seem to have a runny nose/cold   yes/no

If you have answered 'yes' to eight or more of the statements above, then it is possible you have a food intolerance – but this questionnaire cannot confirm whether or not this is the case. The only way to be sure is to consult a qualified nutritionist who can arrange for a biochemical test to assess food intolerance, yeast sensitivity and the levels of gut flora – the 'friendly bacteria' that live in our intestines – as well as the condition of the mucus lining of the intestinal walls. A low level of gut flora, problems with the mucus lining of the intestinal walls and excessive intestinal yeast add up to intestinal permeability – better known as leaky gut! – which in turn can provoke intolerances to other foodstuffs.

Medical science is not 100% certain why food intolerances occur but it is widely believed that continually and repeatedly eating the same food can in part be responsible for their development. The main foodstuffs that have been identified as the worst offenders are:

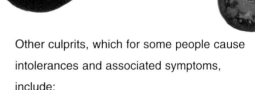

wheat
glutinous grains (such as oats,
  barley and rye)
dairy products
yeast
sugar
corn
alcohol

Other culprits, which for some people cause intolerances and associated symptoms, include:

eggs
citrus fruits (except lemons)
the nightshade family (tomatoes,
  potatoes, peppers
  and aubergines)
soya products

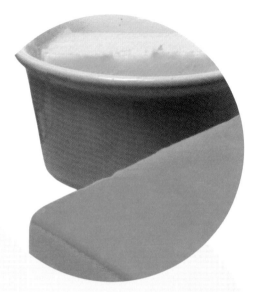

One look at the list of troublesome foods –
pretty much what we eat each and every day
– makes sense of the idea that a food
intolerance develops from the continuous and
repeated eating of particular foodstuff.

Consider just how much and how often we
eat wheat in one form or another – as
cereals for breakfast, in bread, cakes and
biscuits, as pasta, as well as in disguised
forms: just take a look at the list of
ingredients on processed foods and ready
meals and you'll find wheat!

many of the foods that can
adversely affect us are those we
have always eaten regularly.

Because we've always eaten wheat – or
eggs, or dairy products – and because unlike
an allergy – we have never experienced any
immediate and acute reactions – we have
assumed that our bodies are quite happy
putting up with these foods. The reactions
we do suffer – headaches, upset bowels,
bad hair days – because they come a couple
of days later, we assume must be caused by
something else. Only when we cut out the
wheat, eggs or dairy products do the
symptoms disappear.

Most of us are afraid to eliminate the foodstuffs on the list of possible suspects because a) they are familiar, readily available, and we like their taste and b) we have this notion that without just one of these items, at the very least we won't be eating a 'healthy balanced diet' and at the very worst, we'll become malnourished and starve to death! It wouldn't be much fun wearing the same outfit of clothes everyday – even if it fitted well, and was always cleaned and pressed, ready for us to put on each day – and the same is true of food. Just because we've always eaten this or that thing, doesn't mean we must carry on eating it. And, just because you find you never eat one thing again, it doesn't mean you won't eat something else in its place. In fact, during the three week detox, you will be eating three meals and two snacks each day, as much fruit and vegetables as you like, and, unlike many other 'diets', you will be the one deciding what the portion sizes are.

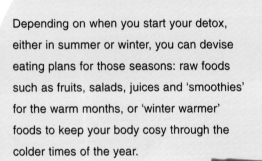

Depending on when you start your detox, either in summer or winter, you can devise eating plans for those seasons: raw foods such as fruits, salads, juices and 'smoothies' for the warm months, or 'winter warmer' foods to keep your body cosy through the colder times of the year.

unfortunately it often seems like it is the most enjoyable foods that are the main culprits.

the detox foo

whatever the season, the foods you will be eating will not only assist

your body in the elimination and cleansing process, but you will also

be nourishing it with fibre-rich, nutritional, antioxidising and energy-

giving foods.

water

Drinking lots of water is an important part of detoxing: as it sweeps through the body it cleanses and eliminates the accumulated toxins within it and keeps each of the vital organs working efficiently. The minimum amount of fluids required by the body each day is 1 ½ l (1 ½ quarts) in order merely to replace what is lost 'naturally'.

dstuffs

juices

Freshly made vegetable juices are a vital part of detoxing because they are both highly alkaline forming and are packed full of antioxidising nutriments and enzymes.

The average diet is generally made up of acid forming foodstuffs such as meat, eggs, dairy produce, alcohol and some grains such as wheat. Diets high in such foods put a great strain on the digestive system, making elimination difficult, and deplete your energy levels. Think of how often after a large meal – pasta with a meat sauce, a liberal sprinkling of cheese and a couple of glasses of wine for instance – how 'low' we feel – tired, heavy headed or even depressed. Our bodies, in fact, prefer the exact opposite types of food – those that are alkaline forming like fruits, vegetables and juices to give us energy that lasts longer than the quick 'high' given by a chocolate bar, which is inevitably followed by a rapid 'low'. Antioxidants are the storm force when it comes to searching and destroying the unwanted wastes and toxins in the body, while foods that are unprocessed and unadulterated by chemicals keep their original, high enzyme and nutritional values.

A glass of vegetable juice – carrot juice for example – will take about 500g (1 lb) of fresh, and wherever possible, organically grown, carrots to make. So in one easy-to-drink glass you will drinking a highly concentrated source of unadulterated, natural, alkaline forming, antioxidising and enzyme rich nutrition.

fibre rich foods

We all know the value of a diet high in fibre,
yet few of us actually do anything about
increasing the amount we eat. And even
when we do, we tend to opt for wheat bran.
Not only is it tasteless, wheat bran, because
the fibre is insoluble, is often difficult to digest
and can cause irritation in the digestive tract.
During detox, fibre is provided by fresh fruit
and vegetables, which unlike bran, is soluble
and a far gentler 'cleanser' of the intestines,
especially the colon.

what to expec

Detoxing is NOT a weight loss programme: this is because there are no restrictions on the quantity of food you can eat. In fact you can eat as much as you want, it's the 'quality' – the nutritional benefits of the foods – that is important. Because you won't be getting any of those 'empty calories' from biscuits, chocolate bars, soft drinks, crisps and alcohol, you may find that you do in fact shed a few pounds. It is also possible that in eliminating certain foodstuffs which are responsible for a particular food intolerance, you find you lose a little weight as well. Most of the time you will be shifting excess fluid rather than 'burning' fat.

Because detoxing is gentle, there are relatively few side effects – in fact you may not experience any of the adverse effects associated with 'reducing' or slimming diets – such as tiredness, mood swings and headaches – at all. With all the gentle intestinal 'sweeping' from the fibre rich foods, and from drinking plenty of water, fruit and vegetable juices, you will find you may have to make more frequent trips to the loo! This is one of the best things that can happen: your body is gently removing all the old accumulated residue and toxins from the digestive tract. It's quite normal to have loose stools at the beginning of your detox while your body adjusts, and don't be alarmed by any colour changes! Vegetables, such as carrots and beetroots, and dark greens, such as broccoli, may cause these colour changes.

detoxing is not about losing weight.

On the other hand, if you have eaten a diet of highly refined, processed foods for a long time, don't be surprised if you suffer from constipation for a couple of days! In this instance, don't use a laxative! Over the counter laxatives not only remove the 'obstruction' but strip the body of vital minerals, leaving it in a weakened state. Instead, try some of nature's own laxatives – 2 or 3 soaked prunes or even a small glass of prune juice – you won't need much! Syrup of figs, chewing a little liquorice root, a very little stewed rhubarb, an infusion of flax seeds, and rose hip tea, are all gentle laxatives and you will find 'recipes' for these and other herbal infusions, teas and juices later on this book. You can also try increasing your intake of Vitamin C – in supplement form or just by eating a little more fresh fruit.

you will find you are eating plenty – just reducing the number of empty calories.

It is important that you 'listen' to what your body is telling you. If you experience tiredness, or a headache, don't be alarmed: this is particularly common after giving up stimulants such as caffeine. It's quite likely that you were tired before you gave up tea and coffee, but refused to acknowledge it and had another cup to keep you going! You will find some very simple but effective self help techniques for headache and tension relief later on, so you won't need to resort to over the counter or prescription drugs.

light, nutritious snacks can be vital to maintain health.

Feeling light headed, vague, or a little 'spaced out' can also be common. It is vital that you eat at least three meals a day and snack between them! This is in order to maintain a normal blood sugar level in the body. A great tasty snack between meals is a rice cake with a little hummus spread on it plus a few carrot sticks or a banana which will give you a complex carbohydrate food combined with a little protein. Remember detoxing is gentle: don't rush it and try cleaning out the complex and marvellous thing that is your body, you will just be punishing it. Take it easy! When you feel light headed, sit down, relax, and have a little snack!

headaches or tiredness are quite common when you have given up stimulants.

Other physical 'symptoms' that are commonly experienced during detox include a 'fuzzy' or coated tongue, a little bad breath or a 'bad' taste – sometimes a coppery taste – in the mouth and feeling that you are a little bit more smelly in general! All of these will pass in time: it's just your body eliminating toxins out through all possible exit points!

More frequent bathing and showering are the simple answer as well as teeth brushing – paying attention to the gums – and, if you wish, using a tongue scraper – or even gently brushing your tongue will help alleviate the effects. A gentle gargle with a mild solution of bicarbonate of soda (2 teaspoons mixed in a little water) is also a highly effective mouth treatment.

paying attention to your teeth and gums will help eliminate bad taste or breath.

You can also expect some non-physical effects as well: while we detox our bodies, we are also detoxing our emotions. Don't be surprised if some feelings or emotions that were kept subdued or suppressed start to come to the surface. Like the toxins in our bodies, these emotions need to escape too! Not everyone experiences emotional effects, or 'moods' – whatever you want to call them, and not everyone will experience them to the same degree or the same way. It is quite probable that as you start to feel physically 'better' your emotional experiences are only positive ones. Congratulations! Perhaps your emotions will go a little up and down – but

hey, what's new? Every emotion is worth experiencing: if you feel blue or low, it could be that your blood sugar level has fallen rather than that you are having an emotional crisis! On the other hand, detoxing for some can bring old emotions up to the surface: let them out. If you feel a little tearful, find a place and have a cry! You'll feel better afterwards – and your eyes will have enjoyed a good cleanse as well!

detoxing is also a time when a little 'emotional cleansing' takes place!

chapter 2

mind &
body
in balance

mind & body

Cleaning out the body – getting rid of unwanted and unnecessary wastes

and harmful toxins – will do wonders for the way your body looks and

functions, but a great body and a dull, sluggish or burdened mind or

spirit is of little use. Detoxing, as mentioned earlier, is all about achieving

'balance' – or harmony, or peace or whatever you wish to call it.

lots of 'conventional' diets
don't take into account the
fact that our emotions and
physical wellbeing are linked.

balance

Most ordinary diets – those 'slimming' or 'reducing' diets with their strict regimes of calorie counted, portion controlled meals and fat burning exercises – rarely, if at all, take account of our emotions, moods, feelings, or desires. These diets most often fail to take account of the fact that our bodies are the 'vehicle' which carry these feelings and our minds are the 'engines' that drive and motivate the body. Too often we embark on a rigorous diet that punishes the body for apparently 'misbehaving' – it's not working properly or it's not looking good. In short, we take out our 'feeling bad' on our bodies – which are simply telling us that we aren't happy by sending us visible bodily signals in the hope that we'll take notice!

pampering yourself is a surefire way to improve both your physical and mental wellbeing.

Detoxing is different: it allows you to take account of those inner feelings, to acknowledge them, to deal with any uncomfortable or burdensome ones, and to make use of the positive ones. Feeling glum, or fed up? Got the blues? Sick of your daily routine? Take a look in the mirror and you'll see all these reflected in your body: your eyes aren't sparkling, your hair is dull, you've got a spot or two, you feel fat or bloated, your back is 'slumped', your mouth is turned down at the corners instead of upwards and smiling. It's quite normal to feel this way and your body is sending you the signals of being fed up too! But instead of punishing your body – it's not its fault, honest! – give it a break: nourish the insides with lovely fresh foods and pamper the outsides with long, luxurious scented baths, and tackle the reasons why you are feeling fed up! Dealing with these will make more space for the important feelings and emotions: all the good things about yourself, your life, your world and the people in it you care about, and you will actually see these positive feelings the next time you look in the mirror.

Too often we make 'life changing' decisions when we are feeling at our lowest of low points, physically and emotionally – when we've got an illness and look and feel terrible, when a close relationship has ended, when we've had an argument with a family member, friend, colleague or boss at work. This is probably the worst time to make any major decisions at all: they seem huge and nearly impossible. But we still make these decisions because we know, deep down, that if these life changing decisions don't work out well, we can always blame someone else – the person who gave us the flu, the ex-partner, the boss or even a relative. All this does is continue the cycle and makes us even more bitter about the 'hurt' we experienced in the first place and fills us with feelings of regret.

times of stress or when we're feeling at our lowest, are not the best times for making life changing decisions.

At these points in our lives, it is the time to concentrate on feeling better physically and emotionally – to allow ourselves to heal. And when that has been achieved, we can sit down and calmly, carefully and in our own time and to our own timetable, think about what we want to change and how we're going to make those changes. In short, we can make any changes when we are in 'control'. It may sound a little self-centred or even selfish, but acknowledging what we want, what we truly desire, and what we need, means that the decisions and changes we make will be the right ones, and come at the right time, for us.

we need time to relax and heal ourselves before making big decisions.

restoring the mind and body balance

During a detox programme you'll be nourishing and cleansing your body and getting back 'in touch' with it – finding out what it needs, what it likes, what makes it 'better' – so now is a great time to do the same with your mind and spirit. Some of the things you can do include some simple yoga or tai chi exercises, as well the relaxation, self massage and reflexology sequences. These are all easy, yet effective methods of getting back in touch with your body and bringing about a more balanced mind-body relationship. You'll also find affirmation and visualisation techniques and benefits explained so you can relate these to your goals, your needs, and your desires.

many of the techniques that
follow are excellent for
balancing mind and body.

the daily deto>

Use your detox journal to write down not only your physical responses to the detox experience, but your moods, feelings or emotions as well. By writing down these inner thoughts you'll find you will have released them – you are not 'dwelling' on bad feelings and they're not burdening you emotionally and physically.

ournal

Write down the good feelings you have as well, and for each feeling, try to identify what it was that made you feel this way. It may be a person, a place, a task, a smell, a taste – anything! It may surprise you just what you respond to! By writing these down in your detox journal, you have a record of the things that give you pleasure – so you can do them again – and the things which you didn't like, so you can avoid repeating them or even eliminate them from your 'diet' – your 'way of life'. Your detox journal can be your own private space: don't feel silly or embarrassed by the things you write. Some of those feelings will diminish or even disappear completely later on – but at that moment when you wrote them down, they were your true and real feelings at the time. If you can't find words to express how you feel, why not sketch it instead, or find a colour, a texture, a pattern – a brightly coloured sweet wrapper that made you smile; a piece of fabric that brought back memories, or even a leaf or flower – put it in your journal to remind you. Let your detox journal become an album of your feelings.

writing about your feelings, and their causes, can be cathartic. Or collect items that represent those feelings, whether a flower, pattern – anything.

time isn't mo

We have all been brought up to think that time is money: we talk about 'saving time', 'spending time' and admonish ourselves and others for seemingly 'wasting time'. Well, it's time to start thinking about time in a different way. You can't go to a time bank and deposit a couple of seconds, minutes or hours – squirrelling them away for when you're short of time! You can't withdraw some of those seconds or minutes! You can't spend time like money and, thinking like this, it is actually impossible to waste time! Every moment is 'used' – and the more these moments are enjoyable, the better!

time isn't like money – you can't
withdraw extra if you need it!

The gradual passing of the day – from lightness to darkness; the gentle change in seasons; the growth and development of our bodies – are all 'part of nature' and nature is a smoothly flowing process where the change from one state or condition happens gradually. We may notice the changes in the seasons – the leaves turning golden and falling from trees, the changes in our bodies from youth to maturity, the beautiful light of dawn or dusk – but there is no exact moment 'in time' we can truly pin down when this happens. We don't wake up one day and suddenly we are 'adult' – maybe in legal terms we are because we have reached a certain birthday, but our bodies or minds may be at a completely different life stage; not all the leaves fall off the trees on the same day, and the times of dawn and dusk and the way

they look are different over the time this magical process happens. Because 'nature' is constantly 'flowing' from one stage to the next, to 'make sense' of it, we gave names to the seasons, divided the year into manageable months, the months into weeks, and then into even smaller divisions of days, hours, minutes and seconds. What we have done is made 'categories' of nature, and given them names. We have made a construction called 'time' but we often allow this construction to rule our lives: we watch the clock at work through the day; we count the days until the weekend or holiday; we yearn for a moment's rest.

we see changes in nature occur gradually – leaves go brown, but we cannot pinpoint the exact moment it happens.

in the same way we can't predict or pinpoint exactly when we change from youth to adulthood – time is a flowing concept.

take the time to recreate
relaxed moments at regular
times: listen to your favourite
music. This is not wasting time,
it's taking time for yourself.

Think about how you compartmentalise time every day, and then think back to your last holiday and how different you felt. Was it possibly because you 'spent' your time differently, or perhaps because you made 'time' itself less of a fixed routine.

or, think of something that makes you smile while in a queue.

Since we have compartmentalised our 'regular' lives into these hours, minutes and seconds, any opportunity to 'rest' – an opportunity to regain those very feelings you enjoyed on holiday – that doesn't come 'at the right time' is regarded as 'wasting time'. Instead, we need to recognise these 'moments' and celebrate them: use the time spent in the queue at the bank to think about nice things that bring a smile to your lips; use the time sitting waiting for your turn in the dentist to relax and breathe; use the time on the bus to and from work to read a new novel, or listen to some music, or learn a new language on a personal stereo. Or just use these moments to daydream: let your mind be free of constraints and let ideas flow into it. If you want to make changes to the way you feel and look, then thinking about time is a good place to start. Instead of thinking about wasting, spending, saving or losing time, why not start thinking about 'making' some time for yourself!

time to breath

We all know that if you don't breathe, you die. Breathing is a reflex action – our bodies very cleverly do it all by themselves without any help from us 'consciously' breathing. This reflex action does what it's supposed to do: help the flow of oxygen around the body to the vital organs. Reflex breathing is a tough job because the body is always needing oxygen here or there – and the poor old blood has to get rid of all the waste as well before it can get back to the lungs to be 'refreshed' with new breaths. Because we leave it to the reflexes to breathe, the enormous capacity of our lungs is underused. That spare capacity is there for a reason: for us to fill and help the body and its organs get an even richer supply of that vital oxygen.

Breathing in and out in a deep and controlled way is relaxing because it allows us to find the 'centre' of ourselves so to speak. We spend a great deal of energy 'tensing up', holding in our stomachs which restricts our intake of oxygen to the upper chest only, and consequently, limiting the amount of air allowed to fill our lungs. The more you allow your body to be filled by deep breathing, the less stress you place on your body and subsequently, your mind. The more you practise your deep, controlled breathing, the more natural it becomes and you can call on it at any time of day to help you through those tired or stressed out moments. Soon you won't need to 'feel' the inhalation and exhalation with your hands. Think about the very act of breathing when you are doing it: remember that you are bringing in a life giving force into your body and feel its energy flowing through you and healing you.

Often the only time we are really conscious of breathing deeply is on holiday, when we open the balcony doors and breathe in deeply, the fragrances of the place – the smell of the sea or lakes, of the mountains, of forests and flowers or the desert. Ever wondered why you felt so good on holiday? It's because you're not thinking about 'time' in your usual way, and by breathing in those fragrances, you're breathing deeply, filling your lungs with oxygen that feeds your vital organs. You can repeat that good feeling anytime you want: all you have to do is breathe. If you feel stressed out at work or at the end of a long, hard day and you can't sleep, or if you just want a few minutes to yourself, you'll find this simple breathing exercise really beneficial.

let the energy

There are several methods of improving your energy flow, and balancing

your mind and body. The following are some of the most effective – and

enjoyable – forms.

Make yourself comfortable: you can either sit
down, lie down, or even stand up if you want,
whatever is best for you.

step 1

Breathe in slowly through your nose to the
count of four. Breathe in deeply, so deep in
fact that you feel your tummy expand – not
just your chest.

flow

step 2

Hold onto that deep breath for four counts, then, exhale slowly through your mouth to a count of eight. This slightly longer exhalation means you are expelling all the stale, deoxygenated and no-good air from those nooks and crannies deep in the bottom of your lungs. Now repeat the whole breathing in – right down so your tummy expands, holding, then exhaling 9 more times – it only takes a couple of minutes and then notice how relaxed you feel.

Once you get used to this way of breathing, you can dig a little deeper: leave one hand on your stomach and place the other lightly across your chest. Breathe right down so your tummy expands and when it can't go any further, breathe in some more and fill the tops of your lungs. This time the inhalations and exhalations are the same length – 8 counts each, without holding in between, so the whole process is smooth and uninterrupted. When you exhale, let the old air out from your chest first, then from your tummy – it's obvious, there's no room up top for any more!

qi gong

Qi gong is a Chinese system of 'working with energy'. This sequence of movements – they're too gentle and fluid really to be thought of as exercise – is made up of three parts: joint opening, grounding and closure. As its name implies, the joint opening movements 'open' up the joints in the body, removing stiffness and aches and making them strong and flexible. Opening the joints allows for the smooth flow of energy throughout the whole body and also helps to move wastes and toxins in the body, which often accumulate around the joints, so they can be eliminated.

The grounding movements of the second phase of the sequence are great for balance – both physical and mental – and help to energise both mind and body. The closing sequence may seem – and feel – a little strange the first time you do it: You are 'listening' to your body, feeling the tensions and stresses – the negative forces flowing out of your body and new vitalising forces entering into it. Don't be alarmed if you feel physical sensations or a heightened emotional awareness – or even both! This is good news! Energy is flowing through your body and you are aware of it – perhaps for the very first time. To help you get the most out of the sequence of movements, remember it is not a punishment, a battle or a race: do it at your own pace and let yourself – and your body – enjoy it and benefit from it. Keep your body relaxed and your 'attention' focussed on each part of the body that you 'work' or move through – allow yourself to experience – to feel – the sensations in each part of your body. The movement sequence starts with your feet and moves upwards through your body, right through your neck and head.

step 1

Start off the sequence by standing in the
'basic position':

Take off your shoes and socks and stand
with your feet apart – so they are apart by
the width of your hips – with your toes
pointing straight ahead. Move a little from
one foot to the other just so you distribute
your weight equally over both feet.

Bend your knees slightly, tuck your pelvis
in, underneath you a little – so your bottom
is not sticking out – and keep your spine
straight, but comfortable.

Lift your head so it is upright and keep
your eyes open, but focussed slightly
towards the ground or floor in front of you.

Relax your arms – let them hang loosely
at your sides (sometimes it helps just to
gently 'shake out' your hands).

When you are comfortable and relaxed in
the basic position, move to step 2.

step 2

Lift your left leg so your foot is about 5 cm (2 in) off the floor. Keep both your knees 'soft' – slightly bent. Now gently rotate your left ankle in a clockwise direction 10 times, then anticlockwise 10 times. Replace your foot on the floor, and rebalance your body weight over both your feet. Repeat with right leg.

step 3

Place your hands on your knees and 'cup' them with your palms. Rotate your knees: your right knee making a clockwise, circular motion 10 times while your left knee rotates 10 times in an anticlockwise, circular motion. When you have done these, reverse the direction of each knee and rotate them 10 times.

step 4

Return to a 'standing' position – but with your knees slightly bent – and lift your left leg off the ground by about 30 cm (12 in). Bend the knee on the lifted leg to 90 degrees. Now rotate your knee clockwise 10 times, then anticlockwise 10 times. Replace your foot on the floor, rebalance, lift your right leg and repeat and then return your foot to the floor and rebalance.

step 5

Keeping your knees bent, rotate your pelvis very slowly in a clockwise circular motion 10 times. Really feel your bottom making a circle – and don't be alarmed if you hear any odd noises starting to come from your body!

Repeat in the opposite direction, rotating your pelvis very slowly, 10 times anticlockwise.

step 6

Twist the top half of your body from your waist – first to the left, then back to the middle and then on to the right. Try and make this one slow, continuous fluid movement – don't fling yourself around, instead feel how your waist is 'stretching'. Let your head follow the movement of your spine and your arms flow across and around as you move. Twist 20 times. Every time you twist you'll stretch a little further and soon you'll be able to touch your spine with your furthest fingertips. This movement all happens in the waist – your pelvis and knees remain in place – and try to keep the movement around the waist all on one level – don't bob up and down as you twist and stretch.

step 7

Return to your 'centre' and lift both shoulders up towards your ears, rotate them backwards and downwards, then upwards and forwards, so you make 'circles'. Do 10 circles 'backwards' and then 10 more, making circles in the opposite direction.

step 8

Return to your 'centre' and move your head to the left, over your left shoulder, then back to the middle, then over your right shoulder. Again, aim to make this one slow, fluid movement, keeping the rest of your body still and relaxed. Do 10 of these and don't worry if you can't turn your head 'equally' – to the same extent on both sides – to begin with: it is often because we favour one side of our bodies over the other – think which side you carry a handbag or briefcase on and it's not surprising that the neck muscles on one side are more scrunched up than the other! With practice you'll find that both sides of your body are balanced and both can stretch to the same extent.

step 9

Now return to your 'centred' basic position, and keeping your knees slightly bent, really 'feel' your feet on the ground. If you wish, imagine your feet are sending out roots. Let tension drain down through your body – first out of your head, down your neck, through your spine, down your legs, into your feet and out of your body into those roots in the ground. Stay in this relaxed position for a few minutes and breathe: breathe in deeply through your nose, filling your lungs right down to your tummy and right up to the top of your chest and then exhale slowly through your mouth, expelling all that used up and now useless air. Don't be alarmed if you start to feel warm, or, your legs start to tremble a bit, or, your fingers feel twitchy – that's energy flowing through your body! And don't be alarmed if you don't 'feel' anything at first: give yourself a little time to get used to the movements and to 'hear' and 'feel' your body. After all, it is speaking to you in an unfamiliar language!

step 10

Inhale slowly through your nose, and at the same time, lift your arms out to the sides and over your head.

step 11

Exhale slowly through your mouth and at the same time, lower your arms back to your sides. Repeat this 3 more times.

You can do this sequence any time you feel like it and every day. In summer try doing it in the park or on the beach, feeling the grass, earth or sand between your toes. In winter, you can do it indoors, but you could also take a chance and experience at least once in your lifetime what it feels like to have snow under your bare feet! Wherever you do your sequence, make it a good experience for your mind and your body. Remember, you are nurturing and nourishing them, not doing battle, or punishing them.

tai chi

This ancient Chinese 'system' dates back to 3000 B.C. Tai chi means 'big energy' and as well as being an excellent form of exercise, it also involves becoming aware of both our own personal energy and the energy that surrounds us. This exercise works well after the joint opening and grounding sequence described above, because your energy levels will be quite elevated. You can, however, try it at any time that is suitable for you. You can do this exercise, called chi ball (energy ball) sitting down, but try to keep your back straight and both feet firmly and squarely on the floor. If you prefer to stand, work from the basic position described above. Don't be disappointed if you don't 'feel' anything the first few times you do this: it may take a little time to get used to the exercise and to 'feeling' your body. With practice you will be able to build quite large and quite 'solid' chi balls.

step 1

Vigorously rub the palms of your hands together for 30 seconds.

step 2

Slightly cup your hands and move them about 60 cm (2 ft) apart with the palms facing each other. Bend your arms at 90 degree angles so your hands are parallel to your diaphragm.

step 3

Close your eyes, and very, very slowly, start
to bring your hands together. Concentrate on
the sensations that you feel in the palms of
your hands: this is energy flowing through
them. Keep your eyes closed and let your
hands get closer together: when they are
about 10 to 12 cm(4–5 in) apart you may
start to feel your hands getting warm and
beginning to tingle, and it may feel as though
there is something between them – a tennis
ball perhaps.

Try to visualise a solid ball between your
hands and move your hands around it as if
you were turning a tennis or cricket ball
around. Play with the ball for as long as you
can remain focussed: if you lose the feeling
that the ball is there, rub your palms together,
move your hands a little apart then bring
them together again. Try imagining that the
energy contained in the breath you exhale is

flowing through your arms, into your hands
and into the ball – this helps the ball feel
bigger and more solid – as if you are
breathing life into it.

step 4

When you are ready to finish, place the
palms of your hands gently on your lower
abdomen and take a couple of good deep
breaths. Think the energy from the chi ball
back into your body: feel the heat and the
energy flow into you. When you've
reabsorbed all the energy, shake your arms
vigorously and rub the soles of your feet on
the floor.

yoga

Yoga is possibly the supreme 'exercise', combining and harmonising

meditation with physical fitness to ensure that the mind and body

function efficiently and to their maximum potentials. There are six main

'paths' to Samadhi ("Union"), the goal of yoga: Jnana (union by

knowledge); Bhakti (union by love); Karma (union by service), Mantra

(union by speech), but the two which have the most appeal, especially

in the west, are Hatha (union by bodily control) and Raja (union by

mental control).

Hatha yoga and Raja yoga are most often practised together: Hatha yoga, which consists of physical exercises and breathing practices, is an ancient system for achieving and maintaining bodily health and fitness. Not only does it develop strength of the muscles, but the health and efficiency of the internal organs – the heart, lungs, glands, nerves and so on – also benefit. You don't need any special equipment for Hatha yoga, and it can be 'performed' anywhere you like. Just as Hatha yoga aims at 'mastering' the body, Raja aims at 'mastering' the mind – to gain control over the flow of thoughts, to still the mind by concentration (Dharana) and contemplation (Dhyana). Raja yoga is the means by which we can put our 'mental house' in order and concentrate our energies. As our bodies become cleansed, so too do our minds, and with regular practice, you can build up a store of physical and mental energy that you can draw on whenever you need to.

Learning yoga – or any other subject – from a qualified, experienced teacher is always the best way to become familiar with the techniques, aims and the 'language' of yoga. Each position or 'Asana' has a special purpose, and may take a little time to achieve, but it is important that you are happy, and willing to progress gradually. Remember, just by trying the postures, you will be doing your body and your mind some good.

If you are already familiar with yoga, then put into practice what you already know. If you are a 'new comer' – or don't want to venture into the Raja yoga 'mental' exercise at this early stage, then try some of the following stretches. Remember, it's not a battle!

the cobra

This pose stretches the spine, massages the organs and develops the chest.

step 1

Lie on your front, resting your forehead on the floor and with your feet together. Inhale. Place both palms down flat, near your armpits.

step 2

Exhale. Raise your head slowly, then continue arching upwards, keeping your elbows bent and your stomach on the floor. Hold for six deep breaths and keep looking steadily upwards.

Exhale. Lower your body slowly, release your arms, turn your head to one side and rest. Repeat two or three times, then relax.

cat stretch

This really keeps the spine flexible.

step 1

Kneel on all fours, making sure that your knees are well protected. Begin to curl your spine like a cat's arched back. Exhale. Lower your head and let it hang freely. Round your back until you feel a stretch at the back of your shoulders, and lift your stomach towards your spine. Hold, breathing deeply for three breaths.

step 2

Inhale. Raise your head, pointing your chin very high. Feel your pelvis tip backwards, creating a flexible curve along the entire spine. Hold for three breaths and repeat a few times. Rest.

A more advanced version increases the cat
stretch and flexion of the spine and involves
balancing.

step 1

Kneel on a pad or mat, with hands placed flat
and arms straight.

step 2

Inhale. Extend your right leg backwards and
raise it upwards.

step 3

Lift your head up and hold for three deep breaths.

step 4

Exhale and lower your leg, bringing your head as close to your knee as possible. Hold for three deep breaths. Repeat on the other side.

hamstring stretch

This pose works the legs, creating a long stretch for the hamstring muscles. Because there is a forward bend, the spine and shoulders also benefit.

step 1

Point both feet to the right, clasp your fingers together behind you, squeeze back your shoulders and lift your chest. Lengthen the front of your body and lift your arms.

step 2

Exhale. Bend forward and bring your head to your right knee, raising your arms high behind your back.

step 3

Hold the pose while deep breathing for 30 seconds.

step 4

Inhale. Raise your body upwards, with your hands on your hips.

step 5

Exhale and arch your body into a back bend, squeezing back your elbows to open your chest. Repeat on left side.

relaxation

Every day you should make time to 'do nothing' – in other words, time for rest and relaxation. It may be right at the end of your day before you go to bed – 15 minutes enjoying a good read of a novel or magazine – or during the day, perhaps when you get home from work. While everyone thinks they relax, few of us actually do it consciously. There are many techniques that can be used, but one of the simplest – and most pleasant – is also one of the most effective. If you can, learn to relax for at least 15 minutes and build up to a beneficial half an hour. If you like, light a few scented candles – but make sure they are safe – and put on some soft, relaxing music. Unplug the phone – this is your time!

scented candles can help you unwind.

Take off your shoes, loosen your belt or waistband, and undo any buttons at your neck and wrists. Place a duvet, or blanket with pillows or cushions from the sofa on the floor. Lie down and place one pillow under your thighs, so that your whole back is in contact with the floor; place another pillow under your feet and one to support your head, and one cushion or pillow at either side of you so you can rest your arms comfortably.

Move the pillows or cushions around until you feel really comfortable and all your limbs are supported: they should be raised a little so they are slightly higher than your torso.

Close your eyes and imagine you are lying on a lilo, floating very gently on the surface of a barely disturbed, beautiful swimming pool. Imagine the warmth of the summer sun on your body. Takes some deep breaths in through your nose and then exhale slowly through your mouth. Now just 'float' gently! If you fall asleep, fine. If you don't, you'll still feel completely relaxed afterwards.

On wintry days, try covering your body with another duvet or blanket to keep you snug. Relaxing on the floor means you can angle yourself so you can look out of a window at the sky or tree tops for a while, or, be like a cat, stretched out comfortably, purring contentedly, and catching every bit of the warmth of the sun as it shines through the windows onto the floor!

visualising techniques
can help you

relax

massage

Massage is one of the oldest and most natural types of therapy known but as our society has evolved, we have distanced ourselves from touching until we regard touching and being touched by others as either 'sexual' or as an 'invasion' of our private body space. Nevertheless, we still know the wonderful feeling of being hugged by friends or family – and we know how happy our pets are when they are stroked and 'massaged' by their owners.

it is often a good way to begin with specific area massage – say foot or head, before trying a full body massage.

Well, massage is something we can all enjoy the benefits of. Being massaged professionally is an idea that many people find off-putting: the best way of finding a masseur or masseuse is to contact one of the professional bodies that regulate and train professionals in complementary therapies. You'll find some contact numbers at the end of the book. You'll be able to find a qualified and professional therapist working in your area. You might find that before you go for a 'full body' massage, you prefer to start with say hand, foot or face massage. This is a good way to build up a relationship with your therapist, and a professional therapist will not push you into undertaking any treatment you are not comfortable having. You could even enrol on a training course yourself to find out more, or, you could introduce your mind and body to massage by doing it yourself – to yourself.

touching someone you love, whether family member, friend or even a pet, can be amazingly therapeutic.

Massage is often confused with aromatherapy, often thought of as a pleasant smelling massage! In fact they work in very different ways: massage is designed to improve circulation through the physical use of different 'strokes' in a variety of pressures, speeds and lengths, while aromatherapy is designed to encourage the body to absorb the essential oils which then trigger effects inside the body. Both are valuable therapies offering great benefits, and whenever possible, you should indulge yourself!

the techniques of aromatherapy and massage are designed to different ends. Aromatherapy massage encourages the body to absorb the beneficial oils.

self massage is invaluable during detoxing.

Self massage is very useful during a detox – and at any other time – because it increases the body's circulation which then helps the efficient flow of lymph. Furthermore, massage can help relieve muscle soreness and release tension, and it improves skin tone, lowers your heart rate and relaxes your mind.

You can use self massage to treat headaches, or to pamper yourself. Why not try a hand massage using salt and olive oil? As with Dry Skin Brushing (see page 180), all the strokes you use in massage should be towards the heart and the strokes should be made using the flat of your hand – fingers together and palms down – or just with the ends of your fingers, but do beware long or scratchy nails! Start all your self massage with light, gentle pressure and very slowly build up to a firmer, quicker pace, but don't inflict pain on yourself! Make sure your skin is nicely warmed up before you start making any deeper strokes or you'll just end up bruising yourself.

Get yourself in a comfortable position and make sure the place you are working in is warm and relaxing too – play some music if you like, or light a few scented candles.

You'll generally need massage oil, but you can also use a little olive, nut or seed oil, a little baby oil, or your favourite body lotion or cream. This will allow your hands to work easily over your skin without slipping or dragging on it.

headache relief massage

You won't need any 'oil' for this and you can do it at work – it's ideal for getting rid of those 'heavy heads' brought on by stress, noise, fluorescent light bulbs and too long seated at the computer screen. It's also a lovely way to wind down at night – especially after you've cleaned your face and removed any makeup. Furthermore, you won't have to take a headache pill that your liver will have to deal with!

Breathe deeply and slowly through your mouth as you massage – if you can, release even more tension by making some deep 'ahhhh' sounds as you exhale – it's the closest we humans get to purring like a cat!

a simple hand massage is an effective way to release tension – and pamper your hands too!

step 1

Place your middle fingers parallel to your eyes –
about 3 to 5 cm (1–2 in) away and just above
your cheekbones. Using firm but gentle circular
motions, massage for 1 minute.

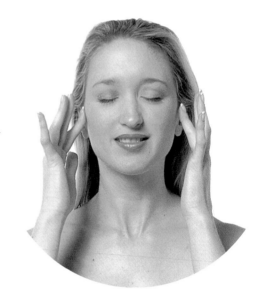

step 2

Move your thumbs along the underside of your
eyebrows – along the bone that is the top of
your eye socket. Feel where this bone meets
the bridge of your nose and close your eyes.
Feel for a point where there is a small
indentation and with very gentle pressure
press your thumbs into the points. Hold for 10
seconds and then release, then repeat again,
three more times.

step 3

Move the middle fingers of your hands to the back of your head and feel at the base of your skull for the point where the top of your neck meets the base of your skull. Using gentle circular movements, massage this area with your finger tips for 1 minute.

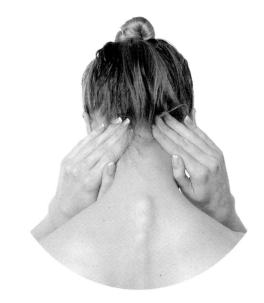

step 4

Now place the palms of your hands on the top of your skull, and gently massage your scalp for 1 minute. When you've finished take a few good deep breaths. If it helps to relieve any remaining ache, lift your shoulders towards your ears, hold them there for 5 to10 seconds, then let them drop back down into their natural position. You can do this a couple of times and you'll feel how your neck feels lengthened and your head feels less weighty.

Hand Massage

This is a real treat for tired hands. Although we use them constantly, it's surprising when you massage your hands just how stiff and tense they are! You'll need some sea salt – but you can use ordinary salt as well – some olive oil, and ideally, a pair of cotton gloves to keep your hands nice and warm afterwards and to let your skin soak up the lovely oil. You can buy cotton gloves quite cheaply and easily from pharmacists – but a pair of clean cotton socks worn as mittens also work just as well! A good time to do this is last thing at night before you hop into bed: that way you can leave the oil on your hands overnight to do its softening magic. The salt gently sloughs away dead cells and leaves your skin smooth and soft, the olive oil moisturises and the massage action increases the circulation. You can add a drop or two of an essential oil if you like as well.

Mix
1 tablespoon of
sea (or ordinary) salt
with ½ tablespoon of
olive oil – and a drop o
two of essential oil if
you wish.

step 1

Scoop up the mix with both hands, and gently rub together. Work slowly at first and build up gradually into a firm 'wringing' motion. Leave the salt and oil mix on for 1 minute, then rinse off with tepid water. Don't dry off your hands – leave the slightly oily residue on and now dip your fingers into a little 'neat' olive oil.

step 2

Wring your hands as though you were washing them – spread the oil all over. Now lean your left thumb into the wrist area of your right hand, and using small circles, gently massage the whole wrist and top of the right hand.

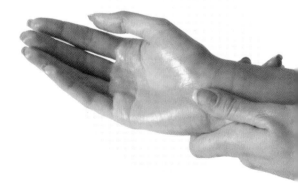

step 3

Place the heel of your left hand over the top
of your right hand, opening out your fingers.

step 4

Lean your left thumb down between each
bone on the right hand and drain towards the
wrist.

step 5

Now lean your left thumb into the back of
your right hand and gently move the flesh
around in small circular movements.

step 6

Turn your right hand over, and lean your left thumb into the palm. Moving over the whole palm in small circles in an upwards and outwards motion, massage the palm and the ball of the hand.

step 7

Repeat the whole sequence, massaging your left hand with your right. When you've finished, squeeze your hands together, give them one final wring and then stretch out each finger in turn. Rub the palms of your hands together to finish the sequence, then pop on your gloves – or socks – notice how warm your hands feel, and get comfy, ready for a lovely night's sleep.

Once you've tried self massage, you really get to like how it feels. It doesn't take long to do and soon you'll be yearning for more. If you can't splash out on a regular massage with a professional, qualified practitioner, then complement and supplement your regular routine with some – or all – of these:

face and neck self massage

Using just the fleshy pads of your finger ends, and with your fingers held together, press onto your face, gently but firmly. Working both hands at the same time, circle both upwards and outwards and down all over the surface of your face: make sure you cover the bony bits as well as the more fleshy bits! Now relax your jaw – we may think it's relaxed but here's how to tell: Is your tongue against the roof of your mouth? If it is, then you are not relaxed! The best jaw relaxing exercise is simply to open your mouth and let your tongue loll out – and don't worry if you drool a little! When you have successfully relaxed your jaw, you can close your mouth and continue to massage in gentle strokes down your neck – front and back – and over your chest. When you've finished, relax your jaw once more.

shoulder and arm self massage

Place your right hand flat on the lower left arm, and keeping as much of your hand on your arm as you can, use firm, long strokes up from the wrist to your shoulder. Keep the pressure on the upward stroke, and release the pressure on the downward ones so you are moving the blood towards your heart. Repeat on the other arm and shoulder.

hand and wrist self massage

Place your left thumb on the knuckle of your right thumb and in long, smooth strokes, 'drain' the blood and lymph to your wrist. Repeat on all the knuckles of your right hand and then change over and massage the left hand.

stomach and chest self massage

You may want to lie down to do this, but you can do it standing or sitting as well. Place your hands flat on your stomach: move your right hand anticlockwise and your left hand clockwise, at the same time, making large circles with firm strokes over your chest and stomach.

lower back and spine self massage

Stand with your legs shoulder width apart and with your knees 'soft' – slightly bent. Put your hands on your hips – with your fingers at the front and your thumbs on your back.

Press your thumbs firmly into your spine and lower back and move in small circles, covering as much of your lower back as you can reach comfortably.

thigh and bottom self massage

This is great for increasing circulation, and toning up those 'problem' areas so often prone to cellulite. Sit on the edge of a bed, place one leg on the bed and support it with pillows, or stand with one leg raised on a chair, and using the flats of your hands, make firm circular movements all over your thigh and bottom. When your skin starts to glow pink and feels warm, make a fist with one hand and continue making circles, working gently at first and gradually increasing the pressure.

a treat for feet

This sequence is derived from Reflexology, a therapy which dates as far back as ancient Egypt and which is based on the idea that there are reflex points or zones on the feet which relate to 'points', organs and systems in the whole body. By 'working' these points or zones on the feet, reflexologists can treat imbalances or illnesses in and of the whole body. It's a little difficult to give yourself a complete reflexology treatment, so you may prefer to have a friend help you – this will also help you relax!

If you feel the benefits, you may be encouraged to seek out a qualified, professional therapist who will be able to offer you a fuller, more complete treatment.

To 'do your own' reflexology, you'll need a large bowl – big enough for you to get both your feet into – filled with warm – not hot – water; a towel to dry off; massage oil – or baby oil or olive, nut or seed oil, and if you want to remove rough skin from your heels – a common occurrence especially in summer when sandals are worn – a pumice stone or emery board. A pair of clean cotton socks are also needed if you don't want to wash off the moisturising massage oil. As with the Salt and Oil Hand Massage (see page 112) you can leave the oil on overnight to be soaked in by your skin.

a little olive, almond, baby oil, or any seed oil, can be used as a massage oil.

Start off by sitting relaxed, soaking your feet in the warm water for five or ten minutes. The warmth of the water will increase the flow of blood to your feet and soften the skin. You can use the pumice stone or emery board to remove any stubborn, dry or coarse skin. Dry off your feet thoroughly, especially between your toes. The following sequence shows one person working on another's feet.

step 1

Sit comfortably and apply a little oil to your hands – rub them together to warm the oil and spread it evenly. Take hold of one foot with both hands and gently clasp it for about a minute. This initial contact helps to relax and reassure your partner.

step 2

Using both hands, stroke the whole foot firmly, covering the top, the sides and the sole of the foot. Work up from the toes, gliding around the anklebones, and return your hands to the starting position.

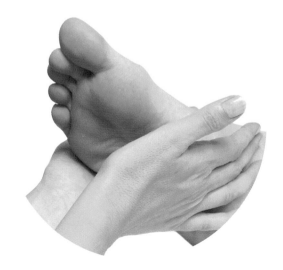

step 3

Hold the foot with both hands so that your thumbs are placed flat against the sole and your fingers are flat on top – one hand will be slightly higher than the other. Pull your thumbs away and past each other towards the edges of the foot, and then allow them to slide back towards each other. Work from the base of the heel up, and back again.

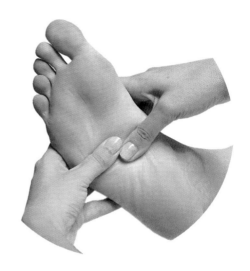

step 4

Interlock your fingers and place them on the top of the foot. Place both of your thumbs at the base of the heel and slide them up to the top of the foot.

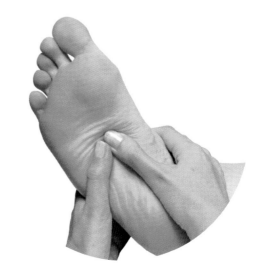

step 5

Cup the heel of one foot so that it is resting in the palm of one hand. With the heel of the other hand, stroke firmly down the inside of the foot, working from the big toe towards the heel.

step 6

Hold the top of the foot with one hand just below the base of the toes. Your hand should wrap around the foot, with your thumb on the sole and your fingers on the top. Make a fist with your other hand and place it on the fleshy area on the ball of the foot. Work from the ball of the foot to the heel, using a gentle, circular motion. This technique helps to soften the tissues on the sole of the foot.

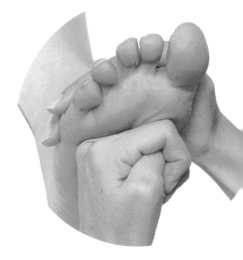

step 7

Place one hand on the inside of the foot and the other on the outside. Using the heels of your hands, pull the outside of the foot towards you with one hand as you push the inside of the foot away from you, and vice versa. Work along the edges of the foot from the heel to the toes and back again.

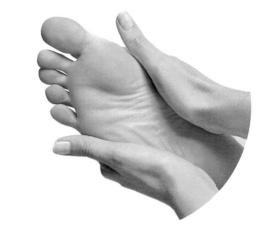

step 8

Support the foot under the heel with one hand, and place the fist of your other hand on the heel area. Slide it slowly from the bottom of the foot to the tips of the toes.

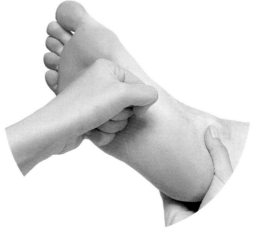

step 9

Support the heel in one hand, with the thumb on the outside of the ankle and the fingers on the inside. Grasp the top of the foot with your other hand and then slowly and gently rotate the ankle several times in one direction and then in the other.

step 10

Support the foot in one hand and, with the other hand, place your thumb on the sole of the foot with fingers on the top. Rotate all of the toes at once to encourage increased flexibility.

step 11

Using the little finger side of both hands, gently flick them up and down the sole of the foot. This is a very stimulating, energising movement.

step 12

Place the palms of your hands on either side of the foot. Move them alternately and rapidly from side to side, so that the foot vibrates. This movement stimulates circulation and relaxes muscles in the foot, ankle and lower leg.

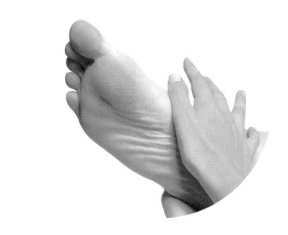

step 13

Support the foot gently with one hand, with the thumb on the sole and the fingers wrapped around the top. Using your other thumb and index finger, gently stretch each toe and then rotate each clockwise and anticlockwise.

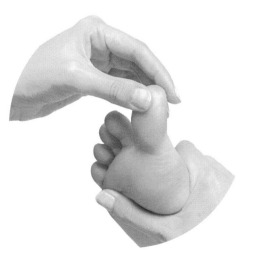

affirmations

Making positive statements about ourselves is not always easy: we are brought up to be 'modest', not to 'blow our own trumpets' and to avoid pride, because, we are always reminded, it 'comes before a fall'. Nevertheless, we yearn for and thrive on the positive things other people say about us: to be told by a boss or colleague that a job was well done, to be complimented for looking great, to be invited to parties because we are good company, or to be told by a lover that the way we smile, crinkle our noses, or walk, is absolutely wonderful. We like to be told these things: they make us feel good, feel alive and valuable and boost our confidence. So why don't we say nice things about ourselves to ourselves? With affirmations you can: they don't have to be 'grand statements', just simple, short things like: 'I have a healthy body'; 'I have a great smile'; 'I feel great' and yes, 'I look great'.

They can also be statements about what you have achieved – over the long term or even just today. Try saying:

'I did some exercises today'; 'I feel energised'; 'Today, I did –' you fill in the blanks as to what you did, what you achieved.

Affirmations can be personal – smiled at someone and they smiled back; about your job or work – a new task or skill you learned; about your home – you spring cleaned or got rid of some excess clutter; a relationship – you started a new one, or, you ended one and will survive; it can even be about money: you spent so much on something and you're really pleased with your purchase, or, you decided not to spend and you're pleased with the money you saved. All they need to be are short statements, but most of all, they must be true.

Once you have made some affirmations about the present, you can start affirming positively for the future. Think of what you want to achieve – in your career, in your personal relationships, in your home, or financially. You don't need to share these affirmations with other people they are yours and yours alone – no-one else need ever know you have made them. Are any of these affirmations suitable for you?

These are just a few suggestions: you decide on what affirmations you want to make and say them three or four times to yourself. Each time you say them, believe in them, and say them with energy, enthusiasm, and true conviction in your beliefs. And most of all smile when you say them: affirmations are there to make you feel good.

I am going to find a better
paid/more interesting/more challenging job'

'I am going to ask him/her out for dinner'

'I am going to save so much money a week and spend
it on a great holiday'

'I am going to end this relationship'

'I deserve and will have more time for myself'

'I can do anything I want,
and I will start doing them

letting go

Sometimes it's hard to move on – in life and in relationships – because we feel held back by our past, by the people in it, and when we do want to move on we feel 'guilty' about wanting to do so. It's hard to let go, and it's hard to let go of all the emotions that we have bottled up inside of us and carried around, letting them and the past cloud the emotions and feelings of the present. Sometimes we can let go of the past a little by getting rid of tangible evidence of it: when a relationship ends we can throw away all the old cinema tickets, the airline stubs, the pressed flowers that were evidence of this relationship. With other relationships – especially those with our family – it's a lot harder to let go. There's no easy way of letting go and moving on, but if you are to fulfil your dreams and desires, and live your life to the full, you either have to let go, or at least be 'at peace' with what has happened in your life.

it can be hard to 'let go' of people who
have played an important part in our lives.

One way you can start is to recognise that all the people – family, friends, lovers, even enemies – and all the experiences, good, bad and indifferent – that you have had, have played an important role in getting you to where you are today. Now you are stronger, fitter and in control. Now you can look back and recognise those people and those experiences for what they have been – experiences.

It may sound a little strange, but now you can 'pay your respects' to those people and experiences – by thanking them for being part of your life.

If there was someone in your life who, for one reason or another, for better or for worse,you need to 'let go of' so you can move on – a parent, a lover, a partner, or even a place that you think the memory or 'hold' over you is still too strong for you to move on with your life and develop further – write their name down on a small square of paper. When you have written down the name, say out loud, 'thank you for having been in my life.' Open the window. Now let go of that person or experience: with a match or candle, light the square of paper and let the smoke carry that place or person's name off into the wider world. That's where it belongs, out there, not weighing you down. It doesn't mean you will forget these people, places or experiences, it just means that when you do think about them, you'll do it in a different way – with a smile.

It's not an easy thing to do: you may not be ready to light the paper and let go completely. Take it one step at a time and when you finally do it – finally thank them for being there at the time – and are truly ready to let go, you will be able to move on unburdened by negative emotions and guilt.

chapter 3

things you
need

things you ne

This chapter concentrates mainly on the food stuffs and related items needed for the detox. You will probably find that you already have most of the things itemised on the following lists in your home: not all of them are compulsory, and with a little imagination and with some of the hints and tips you'll find throughout the book, you'll find you can improvise quite well. However, one or two items are more essential and it's well worth investing in these before you start your detox. Having them ready to hand will make your daily routine a lot simpler.

juicer

A juicer is vital to make fresh vegetable juices. While it is quite possible to buy ready prepared bottled vegetable juices, they can be quite expensive. Furthermore, because they have been mass produced and designed to have an extended shelf life, many of the vitamins and enzymes may have been lost. Preparing your own favourite juice or combining your choices of seasonal vegetables to suit your taste and your body is really the best solution, and the cost of a juicer will soon be recouped because you'll be able to use it long after your initial detox is over. There is a wide range of juicers on the market in a variety of styles – and prices. Remember though when you go shopping, that you want a juicer to make vegetable juice, not a device that only squeezes the juice out of citrus fruits – you can do that quite easily with your hands!

blender

These are ideal for making fresh fruit smoothies in summers and delicious, thick and creamy warming vegetable soups in winter. Again there is a range of styles and prices available, so shop around for the best buy.

coffee grinder/ food processor

Which you buy really depends on the extent of your culinary activities. For the purposes of detoxing, it's the coffee grinder device that's required – although you won't be grinding coffee beans. Instead, you will be grinding flax seeds – an important element in the detox diet. If you don't have a grinder – or don't want to fork out just for that – don't worry: it's not absolutely essential. Flaxseeds can be eaten 'whole' but their goodness is much more efficiently absorbed by the body when they are ground. You could use a mortar and pestle to grind the seeds by hand if you prefer.

thermos flask

Get one and get into the habit of taking a
nutritious lunch to work with you. Wide neck
flasks are useful: you can fill it with soups, or
even rice and vegetable dishes, as well as
cool fruit salads and compotes in summer.

airtight food containers

Get a variety of sizes: big ones, medium
ones and even very small ones. These are
essentially to store fresh food safely and the
different sizes mean you can prepare large
quantities – of rice for example – or use little
containers to store spices and herbs or carry
snacks conveniently around – in your bag,
briefcase or on the car dashboard!

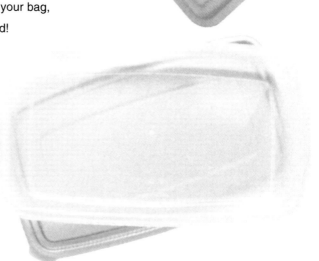

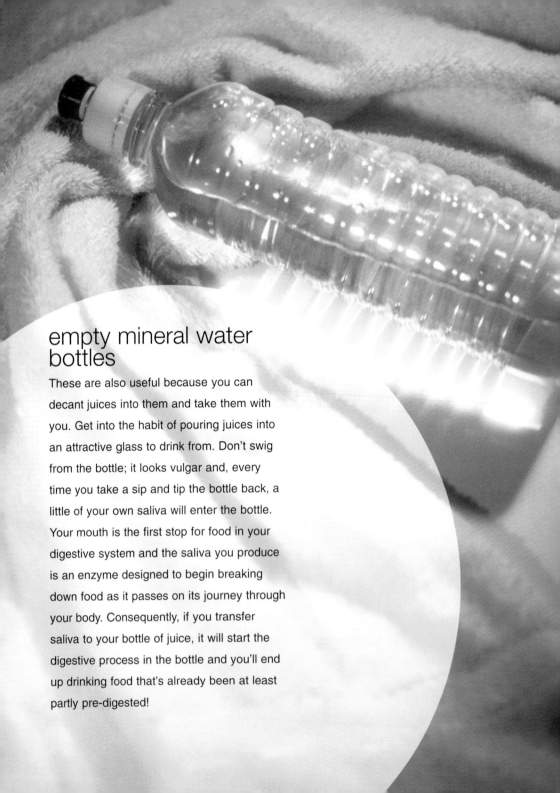

empty mineral water bottles

These are also useful because you can decant juices into them and take them with you. Get into the habit of pouring juices into an attractive glass to drink from. Don't swig from the bottle; it looks vulgar and, every time you take a sip and tip the bottle back, a little of your own saliva will enter the bottle. Your mouth is the first stop for food in your digestive system and the saliva you produce is an enzyme designed to begin breaking down food as it passes on its journey through your body. Consequently, if you transfer saliva to your bottle of juice, it will start the digestive process in the bottle and you'll end up drinking food that's already been at least partly pre-digested!

steamer

This can either be of metal or bamboo. Place it over a saucepan of hot water and steam cook vegetables and fish. Check in the back of your kitchen cupboards – you may find one lurking there already! The bamboo steamer sets are cheap and attractive and food can be served directly from them at the table.

jug water filter

We are indeed fortunate that what comes out of the taps in our homes is of extremely high quality and safe. While you can splash out on bottled mineral water during your detox – but not the sparkling carbonated kinds – tap water is perfectly good. When you buy mineral water, do read the labels carefully and check brands against each other for their sodium (salt) contents. Instead of bottled mineral water, which can be expensive, you could instead invest in a water filter jug – or even two. These will remove some further traces of unwanted chemical substances in tap water, such as lead, copper and aluminium, but you must ensure that the filter cartridge is regularly replaced. If your plumbing is old and made of lead then you really should consider having these pipes replaced. (Depending on circumstances, your local council may be able to offer assistance towards the cost of replacement.) Filter jugs are available in a range of styles: choose one that fits into your fridge easily to provide chilled water, and, a second jug for keeping water at room temperature for cooking.

body brush

Dry brushing your skin will become part of your new beauty regime and many detoxing books recommend you buy a brush made with natural bristles, which can be quite expensive. Natural bristles are in fact tiny hollow tubes of stiff animal hair and they need special care and cleaning to keep them in tip top condition. Wash bristle brushes – including hair brushes – in a solution of warm water, a walnut sized piece of washing soda and a few drops of ammonia. Tap the bristles very gently up and down in this solution but without wetting the roots. Rinse in clean water in the same way and dry naturally, bristles downwards, away from direct heat. It's important to note that because the bristles come from animal sources, if you are a Vegan, or prefer not to use any animal based products, then a plastic bristle brush is perfectly fine. In either case, make sure the bristles are not too hard or stiff and check plastic bristles to see if they have smooth, rounded edges. The brush is for gently exfoliating the skin – not ripping it to shreds!

toothbrushes

Start your detox with some brand new toothbrushes: keep one at home and pop one in a holder in your bag or briefcase for use during the day. Ideally you should replace your toothbrushes every month: not only do the bristles get worn but bacteria accumulate at the base of the bristles around the head! Keep one or two old toothbrushes in your cleaning cupboard: they are useful for dipping into washing solutions and detergents for cleaning around the back of hard to reach places!

tongue scraper

You can buy these from dental practices, pharmacists and many health food stores. The word 'scraper' is a bit misleading, however, because the actual action is in fact a much gentler skimming over the tongue to remove the yucky coating that accumulates. If you are a smoker, a tea, coffee, or wine drinker, or someone who eats a lot of dairy produce or processed foods, find a mirror and stick your tongue out. Chances are it's not pink and lovely, but a rather hideously coloured, slimy coated blob in your mouth that's not fit to lick a stamp! Forget kissing! This is a sign of your body desperately trying to eliminate all the accumulated gunk you've put into it! But one of the side effects of detoxing is a 'coated tongue' and very possibly some bad breath. This is because even if your tongue is lovely and clean to begin with, your body is going to eliminate loads of toxins – in every way it can, and that means through your mouth as well! So be prepared! Some people do find using a tongue scraper uncomfortable: often it sets up a 'gagging' response. This is in fact a very natural – if a little uncomfortable – bodily response. Don't worry, with routine use, this reaction normally subsides. But if you do find that cleaning your tongue with a scraper is too unbearable, try running a very soft bristled, small headed toothbrush – look for a small, children's 'first' toothbrush – along the length of your tongue instead. Get into the habit of cleaning your tongue, and don't be surprised if your dentist compliments you on your improved oral hygiene!

bicarbonate of soda

To me, bicarbonate of soda is a 'miracle powder'. In most homes, a little tub of 'bicarb' will be hidden away at the back of a kitchen cabinet. If it's not actually used for baking, then the only time people remember it is in extreme circumstances – in the middle of the night when they have indigestion! Nothing works better than a teaspoon in a little water. Chances are, if you open your little tub of bicarbonate of soda, the contents are rock solid because the lid wasn't on tightly and the bicarb has absorbed moisture from the atmosphere. Check the 'sell by' date on the carton nd you'll probable find it was sometime last century!

Bicarbonate of soda has a huge number of valuable uses: during your detox, it is used as part of your oral hygiene routine (many commercial brands make a marketing feature of the fact that their toothpaste has 'baking powder' in it) and nothing helps deal with a coated tongue better. You can also add bicarbonate of soda to your bath water to help your body eliminate toxins through the skin. You will need to add about 250 g (8 oz) per bath, but don't exceed more than two 'bicarb baths' a week as it can be debilitating on the body's system. Switch off the phone, light a scented candle or two in the bathroom, make sure the water isn't too hot, and settle back and soak for at least 15 minutes. Afterwards, get cosy, lie down and rest for at least one hour.

Bicarb is also a well known deodoriser, so while brushing your teeth with some will help deal with your breath, sprinkling some in your shoes, boots and slippers will absorb moisture and neutralise those 'cheesy feet' smells that emanate from them! You can dust a little between your clean, dry toes after bathing and some folks even use a little under their armpits instead of commercial deodorants. If you don't fancy this, don't overlook the fact that a paste of water and bicarbonate of soda applied (with an old toothbrush of course) to shirt or blouse collars and underarms helps lift off grime and remove perspiration marks!

somewhere to exercise

You don't need a huge space like a gym, just an area that you can clear away so you can stretch and do your energising exercises. You will find step by step exercises later on in the book: they are easy to follow and execute and build into your daily routine. Remember that these are your exercises for your body – there's no competition so you can go as 'easy' as you feel is right for you. Some days you'll do a really good, long stretch, other days you'll only feel like a little one. But doing them every day will make a difference to how you look and feel. You don't need any special equipment, just some loose comfortable clothing – a tee shirt and sweat pants are ideal.

If you like you can also use a skipping rope: skipping is an excellent method of stimulating the lymphatic system, and is a good aerobic activity for improving general fitness levels. Avoid skipping, however, if you have any back troubles or weak knees. If you live in a flat, skipping is probably not a good idea unless you want your neighbours to hate you! Five minutes skipping outside is a far better bet. The same thing goes for rebounders – mini trampolines. While this is very easy on the body it is also excellent for 'shaking up' the lymphatic system. Take extra care when you 'exit' from the rebounder – don't jump off but slowly step from it to allow your legs and feet to acclimatise themselves to the hard floor surface. Start bouncing gently for five minutes, then build up gradually to a more vigorous bouncing – but take care not to bounce off and that the rebounder stays firmly in place on the floor. Don't improvise by jumping up and down on your bed – it's not the same and the bed always breaks!

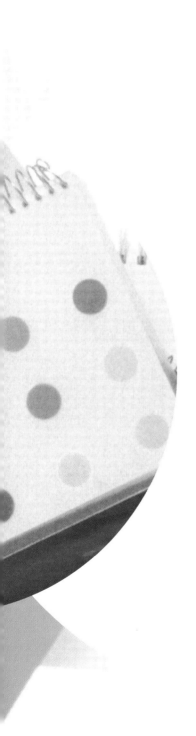

detox journal

Last, but by no means least, don't forget your Detox Journal: get a notebook or diary in which you can keep a daily record of how you feel – both physically and emotionally. Write down any ideas you have about your life, your hopes – and your fears – your thoughts about the past, your feelings about the present, and the future. Writing these thoughts, hopes or worries down releases them from your mind and your body. You won't have to carry them around with you – but they're still there on paper if you want to deal with any issues later on – when you're feeling completely in control and 100% fit.

That's pretty much it for the non-food checklist – apart from the luxurious and pampering bathing and beauty items you'll find in the chapter on body care and daily routine (see page 176), and many of those you can have fun making yourself. The following list is about food and food supplements that you'll need foryour detox.

the detox foo

Detoxing is all about eliminating toxins from your diet – your 'way of life'

which naturally includes the food you eat. Wherever possible – if they are

easily available and if you can stretch your budget, because,

unfortunately, they are a little more costly – buy organic produce.

tuffs

the benefits of organic food

Health food stores, most major supermarkets and even many local, independent traders, now stock organic fruit, vegetables and fish. You won't be eating any red meat so sourcing organic meat is not something you need to think about. However, you may – depending on which detox programme you opt for – be eating a small amount of chicken. This too is available as organic and free range in most supermarkets. Short of leaving your garden uncultivated for at least five years and then growing your own fruit and veg without the use of chemical fertilisers and pesticides, buying organically grown foods is just about the only way to guarantee that all pesticides have been eliminated before the food reaches your mouth. Nevertheless, detoxing is about rebalancing the body and mind and there is no need to become an obsessed 'food fascist': the range and quality of fresh food available to us on a daily basis is astounding and means that we have the luxury of worrying about the quality of the food we eat while much of the rest of the world is desperately concerned with just getting enough of the quantity of food to keep them alive. So, if you want to buy organically grown produce, then fine. If you don't, that's OK too. If you've never really eaten fresh fruit or vegetables, then just doing this will be a radical change of lifestyle. If, on the other hand, they already play a large role in your diet, then upgrading to organic may give your system an extra boost.

the no-no's:

It makes sense to start off by understanding that there are certain things which you will not be eating. During the detox you must avoid:

wheat: and foods which contain wheat – such as bread, cakes, cookies, most breakfast cereals – as well as the other glutinous grains such as oats (sorry, no porridge!) barley and rye.

cow's milk, cheese and yogurt

refined sugar

all meat

oranges, rhubarb and grapefruits

peanuts

dried fruits

shellfish

hydrogenated fats (vegetable spreads)

processed and refined foods – and that includes 'organic' ready meals and quorn products

fried foods (although stir-fry is permitted)

barbecued and burnt foods (grilling and steaming are permitted)

salt (sodium)

coffee, tea (including decaffeinated versions), hot chocolate and malted drinks

carbonated water and other fizzy 'soft' drinks

alcohol (including any 'low alcohol' or 'non-alcoholic' wines and beers)

commercially prepared fruit and vegetable juices: there's really no need because you'll be making your own.

cigarettes (and any other recreational drugs)

Don't be alarmed at this list of no-no's: you will feel and see the benefits. And, to put your mind at ease, here are the things you will be substituting them for and the benefits they offer.

you can have:

In place of wheat, you can have: Rice and rice cakes, and any non-gluten flour, gluten free cereals grains, millet, quinoa, buckwheat and buckwheat flakes, and millet flakes. You can also enjoy pulses (legumes) such as kidney beans, lentils, and chickpeas – which are even nicer when made into hummus. Our typical western diet really means that we should all be eating two or three times more fibre than we are now.

Not too long ago the only thing we needed to know about fibre was that there were two types: soluble and insoluble. Soluble fibre, found, for example, in apples, supposedly lowered cholesterol, while insoluble fibre, found in grains and cereals, didn't, but it did protect against bowel problems, including cancers of the colon. Now we know that, in fact, insoluble fibre, such as that found in rice and bran, also lowers cholesterol. It is thought that it may also relieve gastrointestinal disorders by killing the intestinal parasite Giardia lamblia – commonly picked up from drinking infected water – that may be responsible for the chronic digestive disorder called Irritable Bowel Syndrome, characterised by flatulence, bloating, pain and alternating constipation and diarrhoea. Brown rice is an excellent, and very versatile food: have one portion every other day, alternating with a portion of any of the other grains.

Pulses are not only a good source of complex carbohydrates that provide both energy and essential nutriments, but they also reduce blood cholesterol whether your diet is low fat or high fat! Legumes also contain a so-called 'anti-nutriment' called phytic acid or phytate, the active ingredient which prevents steep rises in blood sugar levels. Phytates are also antioxidants, searching out and destroying the cancer inducing free-radicals. Because pulses (legumes) are acid forming, they do, however, tend to slow down the digestive process, so it's a good idea not to overdo the beans during a detox: one small portion a day is quite enough!

In place of cow's milk and other 'bovine' dairy products, you can have rice milk, nut milk (almond milk is lovely!), soya milk, goat's milk/cheese/yogurt, sheep's milk/cheese and yoghurt. These all have very delicate tastes – not at all strong and smelly – unless of course you like it that way! Chances are you won't really taste the difference, but your digestive system will! You may think it odd that while you can't have cow's milk, you can have other 'milk'. Believe it or not, you may find that in fact you

have a lactose intolerance – and you won't be alone! A large percentage of the world's population cannot drink cow's milk because they lack the enzyme necessary to digest the milk sugars (lactose). Consequently, for many, cow's milk means diarrhoea, bloating, flatulence, abdominal pains and nausea.

On the detox, dairy products are avoided – to give your body the chance to cleanse itself and also to give you an opportunity afterwards to gently 'reintroduce' some products, especially yogurt, back into your diet. Many people do find that they are 'unaffected' by yoghurt made with cow's milk.

goat's cheese

This is because the active bacteria in yoghurt can help correct what is wrong in the stomach and colon, can boost immunity, and even reduce the risk of colon cancer. The 'good bacteria' cultures in 'live' or 'active' yoghurt – Lactobacillus bulgaricus, Streptococcus thermopolis and Lactobacillus acidophilus – continue to multiply in the cosy warmth of the stomach and intestines and create numerous chemical by-products including lactic acid. Consequently, you will find some recipes for smoothies with yoghurt to try. If you do use a cow's milk yoghurt, make sure that it is 'live', and, wherever possible, organic.

Milk and dairy products are suppliers of essential protein: sheep and goat's milk, along with vegetarian proteins found in tofu (bean curd) and quinoa (which has more protein packed into it weight for weight than beefsteak but without the saturated fats, antibiotics and hormones), along with nuts (but not peanuts) will give you as much protein as you need. A handful of mixed nuts and seeds each day and one portion of 'protein food' – fish, tofu, or even a small portion of chicken – are recommended.

canned oily fish is rich in minerals and unsaturated fats.

Dairy products are also a source of dietary fat, but during the detox you will be replacing the saturated fats found in these (and in meats) with unsaturated ones from nuts and seeds, oily fish and cold pressed oil – either sunflower or olive oil. You should also avoid 'ersatz butter', those mass produced 'vegetable spreads' – these may be made from vegetable fats but the process of manufacture makes them high in hydrogenated fats. The 'best' fats are omega-3 fish oils (anti-inflammatory agents which act directly on the immune system to suppress the release of compounds called cytokines that destroy the joints and are thought to be a cause of arthritis) and the monounsaturated fats that can be conveniently and deliciously found in olives, almonds and avocados. As well as being high in stroke-fighting potassium, between 60 and 70% of the fat in an avocado is monounsaturated – heralded for its anti-artery clogging, cholesterol lowering potentials – and moreover, 95% of that monounsaturated fat is oleic acid, an antioxidant which destroys disease causing oxygen free radicals. Also excellent are rapeseed oil and the oil you will be getting from your flax seeds. The point is not to overdose on these alternative fats and oils – especially if you don't want to add unwanted calories – but, if you must eat fat, make sure it's benefiting your body.

avocadoes are nature's pharmacy: high in potassium and a good source of antioxidants.

Flaxseeds are a valuable part of the detox food list: they are very good for the digestive tract and because they don't have a strong flavour they can be added to salads, meals and even to drinks. Furthermore, flaxseeds contain lignans, known anticancer agents.

citrus fruits, such as oranges and grapefruit, should be avoided on detox because they are too acidic and slow down the elimination process.

You can nibble on the whole seeds or grind them up (rather like grinding coffee beans, it's best to grind up just enough for a fresh supply), but keep both seeds and ground seeds in one of your airtight containers in the fridge because heat and light will make them go rancid. You can even soak seeds overnight in a little water: this makes them more digestible and effective.

In place of oranges, rhubarb and grapefruit, and dried fruits you can have ALL other types of fruit, so long as it's fresh. In fact you should celebrate the opportunity not to have to endure the sharp and sour grapefruit – the mainstay of most reducing (slimming) diets! Oranges and grapefruits do contain Vitamin C – but you'll be getting plenty of that! Did you know that just one small radish contains more Vitamin C than you could ever squeeze out of an orange or grapefruit! Rhubarb – which usually has any nutritional value stewed out of it and has to be sugared up to make it palatable in any case – is high in oxalic acid, which in large quantities is toxic. While most of the toxin is concentrated in the leaves – which must never be eaten – the edible stalks also contain it. Dried fruits are not recommended because they inevitably contain E220, or sulphur dioxide, which is used as a preservative. E220 is believed to be associated with causing headaches, nausea and even asthma in some sensitive people. Furthermore, dried fruits are difficult to digest: the only way to make them more

digestible is to soak them in water for prolonged periods to replace the lost moisture content. Why bother with dried out fruits when you can eat fresh, naturally juicy ones with no added chemicals? Don't keep fruits in the fridge – room temperature is best or they'll be too cold on your stomach! You can also stew fruits – a good idea if you've got bargain price punnets or fruit that is going soft or too ripe – chop them up roughly, throw them in a pan with 2 tablespoons of water and heat for 2 minutes. If you find them a little too 'tart' for your taste, add a meagre drizzle of honey to sweeten. Use honey in very small quantities to replace the refined sugar you used previously to sweeten your recipes.

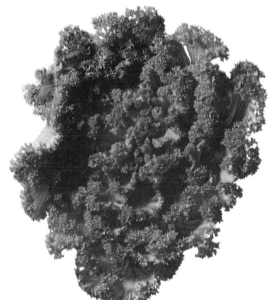

dark green, leafy vegetables are high in carotenoids, minerals and fibre.

All fresh vegetables, because they are alkaline forming, high in nutritional values, fibre and health promoting goodies are allowed. Mixed salads, raw vegetable nibbles for snacks, steamed, baked and stir-fried vegetables also provide flavour and variety. Vegetable juices make for a refreshing change and concentrate all the vital vitamins and minerals into one glass. Have one large glass of carrot juice – made with 500 g (1 lb) of carrots – or try carrot and apple, or carrot and celery, or whatever combination tickles your taste buds – and at least two large portions of vegetables each day. And as many snack nibbles as you want!

the cruciferous vegetables – brocoli, cabbage, sprouts and cauliflower – are well known 'anti-cancer' foods.

If this is your 'normal diet' then it's time to take control!

In place of tea, coffee, chocolate, fizzy drinks and booze, you'll be drinking water – mineral or filtered but never carbonated – along with your fruit and veggie juices. You can also have herbal teas, and lemon water. You must drink a minimum of 1½ litres (1½ quarts) of filtered or bottled still water each day. Some people find it best to set up a 'water schedule': one large glass at 11 am, 2 pm, 4 pm, 6 pm and 9 pm. Get an attractive glass and set the times to suit your own day. Avoid drinking too much water late at night: you'll end up disturbing your sleep because you have to go to the toilet! Avoid drinking too much water with your main meals: it dilutes the digestive enzymes and you want them to be strong and do their stuff! It's also a good idea to wait an hour or so after eating your main meals before you start drinking water again, but with breakfast, snacks and fruit it's fine to drink as you eat.

filtered or mineral water really does taste better when it is 'served' nicely.

One of the most useful detox drinks is the morning lemon juice: the juice of one medium sized lemon squeezed into some water and a slight drizzle of honey will get your digestive system working straight away. In winter, try it hot by making it with a little ginger – a few slices of fresh ginger or a pinch of dried – is warming on a cold day. If you like the taste, don't confine it to breakfast time, drink it throughout the day!

Salt (sodium) not only raises the blood pressure but can also cause damage to the arteries. High-salt diets – common in our society because of the hidden quantities in many processed foods – is also believed to be a contributing factor in osteoporosis because sodium causes calcium loss. Your diet needs to contain twice as much potassium as sodium to create a balanced, healthy flow of nutriments and the efficient elimination of waste. Too much salt and you'll

salt is often one of the 'hidden' elements in our modern diet of highly processed and refined food.

have to boost your potassium intake. You'll have to further increase your intake of fresh vegetables, fruits, beans and seeds! It's better to reduce the level of sodium intake, so the potassium intakes will also be manageable. There are lots of ways you can add flavour to your meals without adding sodium: garlic and celery are great flavours, while herbs and spices will add a 'cordon bleu' finish.

You will, however, be recommended the use of sea salt and Epsom salts as part of your bathing routine as these are an excellent method of removing toxins from the body through the skin. For more information on this, see page 190.

Think about all these foods as a 'food pharmacy', stocked full of healthy goodies:

did you know?

Root vegetables, tubers, fruits, nuts, seeds and grains are high potassium, low sodium foods. Our ancient ancestors thrived on them and now it is believed that potassium rich foods can help combat high blood pressure and protect us from strokes.

Garlic and onions contain substances which help ward off cardiovascular disease, diabetes, infections and cancer. These are highly recommended if you are still smoking (give it up!) or are an ex-smoker. The blood thinning effects of garlic are believed to ward off blood clots – and many people find they are not troubled by mosquitoes on holiday when they increase their garlic intake. Onions – red, white and shallots – are rich in quercetin, a powerful antioxidant and anticancer agent, and are believed to relieve chronic bronchitis and asthma.

Tomatoes, carrots and dark green, leafy vegetables are high in carotenoids, which are vital in preventing the formations of cataracts in the eyes.

Almonds – though high in fat – help fight heart disease because they actually lower the levels of cholesterol in the blood. Other helpful nuts in this area are hazelnuts and pistachios. Walnuts – in nut form or as oil – and sunflower seeds and oil, are full of Vitamin E and are believed by researchers to help in warding off Parkinson's Disease and reduce the severity of the disease for existing sufferers.

Broccoli is an all round winner: it contains a huge range of anticancer agents including beta-carotene, carotenoids, quercetin, indoles (anticancer and great for detoxing), Vitamin C, folate, chromium (anti diabetic and an anti-heart disease agent), readily absorbable calcium (to help prevent osteoporosis and a blood pressure controller) and calcium pectate fibre (to reduce blood cholesterol). Broccoli is also a member of the cruciferous family of vegetables – cabbage, sprouts and cauliflowers – which are closely tied to lower rates of cancer, especially of the colon.

Food for thought? Boost your brain power with boron: foods high in this trace element, which enhances brain function, include nuts, legumes, fruit – especially apples, pears, peaches and grapes – and leafy, green vegetables.

Lycopene, the pigment found in red fruits and vegetables – especially tomatoes and strawberries – helps prevent pancreatic disorders.

You're better off drinking a 100 calorie fresh fruit juice than a zero calorie fizzy drink if you want to lose a little weight! The fructose – fruit sugars – in fruit juices seems to satisfy and suppress the appetite, and, more interesting, the type of foods desired after drinking fruit juices are the less fattening ones!

To fight osteoporosis you don't just need calcium, you need manganese as well. And the best source of manganese is pineapple! Eat it or drink its juice and top up your manganese levels.

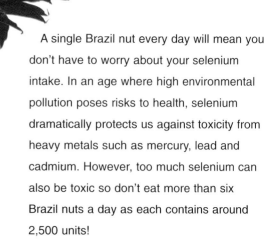

A single Brazil nut every day will mean you don't have to worry about your selenium intake. In an age where high environmental pollution poses risks to health, selenium dramatically protects us against toxicity from heavy metals such as mercury, lead and cadmium. However, too much selenium can also be toxic so don't eat more than six Brazil nuts a day as each contains around 2,500 units!

Mangoes have been found to be superior to commonly used anti viral drugs used against the herpes simplex virus. The compounds found in mangoes stopped the virus from replicating, causing it to die off!

Legumes – chickpeas, soya beans, lentils, red and white beans – are rich in a protease inhibitor called the Bowman-Birk Inhibitor (BBI). This survives both the cooking and digestive processes, and ends up in the colon where it begins its battle against cancer prone cells. It's now believed that the BBI doesn't stop at the colon but instead travels around the body preventing both liver and lung cancers. And by the way, soya beans have double the amount of the BBI than any other legume.

Fresh parsley contains high levels of disease fighting compounds called glutathione which seem to 'switch-off' many cancer causing agents and neutralise some fats which clog up the arteries.

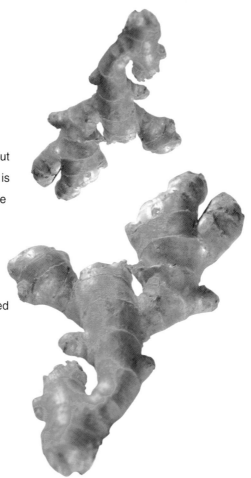

The spice of life: ginger is a strong antioxidant and it's good for seasickness. But did you know that it's also an antibiotic that is very effective against salmonella! Meanwhile thyme – even just the smell of it – has long been used to 'lift the spirits'. In the Middle Ages, inhaling the scent was a remedy for melancholy and epilepsy. Its oil contains a potent antibiotic called thymol – first detected by scientists in 1725 – and is used as an 'expectorant' – it breaks up phlegm in the respiratory tract so it can be coughed up.

So after reading these pages, you now realise that a) you won't starve and b) you'll actually be doing your body a great deal of good. Now you can explore the recipe suggestions you'll find later in this book and plan your menus according to the length of your detox programme.

chapter 4

body
beautiful

body beautifu

With the food elements of detoxing under your belt, you can now move

on to caring for your body. This part of detoxing is not only fun, but

makes a vital difference to how you will look and feel. While the foods

you will be eating will be gently cleansing your body from the inside, you

can devote a little time to cleansing the outsides! This section not only

introduces you to simple but effective daily 'beauty' routines, but also to

some very gentle exercises designed to boost your energy levels or to

help you wind down and relax effectively at the end of the day.

dry skin bru

Not too long ago, advocates of dry skin brushing were regarded as cranks. Today, this simple process is advocated by every health and beauty magazine on the shelves! Not only does it improve the quality of your skin by sloughing off dead skin cells – dead skin cells are dull, while healthy skin cells reflect the light and give the skin that 'glowing' appearance – but it also stimulates the body's production of sebum, a natural, oily secretion of the sebaceous glands, which 'moisturises' the skin. Dry brushing is also an excellent method of improving blood circulation and moving lymph fluids. Improved lymph flow means more efficient elimination of toxins and wastes in the body and encourages new cell growth. You may find that dry skin brushing, particularly around those all too often troublesome areas of thighs, hips and bottom, becomes less of a problem as water retention is alleviated and cellulite is reduced! The entire process of body brushing only takes a couple of minutes each morning, but within days you will see the benefits.

ing

1 you will need a firm but not hard bristled brush – you can use a loofah or loofah mitt if you prefer – but a long handled brush may make it easier to reach those bits between your shoulder blades! Don't wet the brush, loofah, or your skin, or use any moisturiser (you'll be producing your very own anyway!), as this will cause the brush to 'drag' on your skin which can be uncomfortable.

2 strip off all your clothes in the morning and stand or sit in a comfortable position so you can reach all parts of your body. Starting at your feet, stroke the brush or loofah up the front, back and sides of your legs, using long, firm strokes, towards the knees. When you have done your ankles, shins, and calves several times, move up to a knee.

3 stroke up from your knee to the top of your thigh and over your buttock on that side. Then move to the other leg. Move on to your arms, brushing from wrist to shoulder – but treat this area a little more gently – up and over your shoulder and up the back of your neck to the base of your skull.

4 don't dry brush your breasts and remember that your stomach area skin is very delicate, so make sure you use very gentle, circular strokes and work in a clockwise direction – that way you are encouraging the contents of your intestines, which have been lying in your body all night, to move down and along in their natural flow, rather than back the 'wrong way'!

5 you can dry brush your face as well, but it's best to use a soft dry face flannel or a special, soft facial brush. The idea is to slough off skin and encourage circulation, not rip your skin to shreds! Each morning, spend a couple of minutes dry brushing: get rid of all those dead skin cells that got stuck to your body through the night in bed!

6 make sure all the brush strokes move upwards and towards your heart: your heart effectively pumps blood to all the corners of your body, but you can help return the deoxygenated blood against gravity back through the system. (Avoid brushing away from the heart, as this may cause you to feel a little faint).

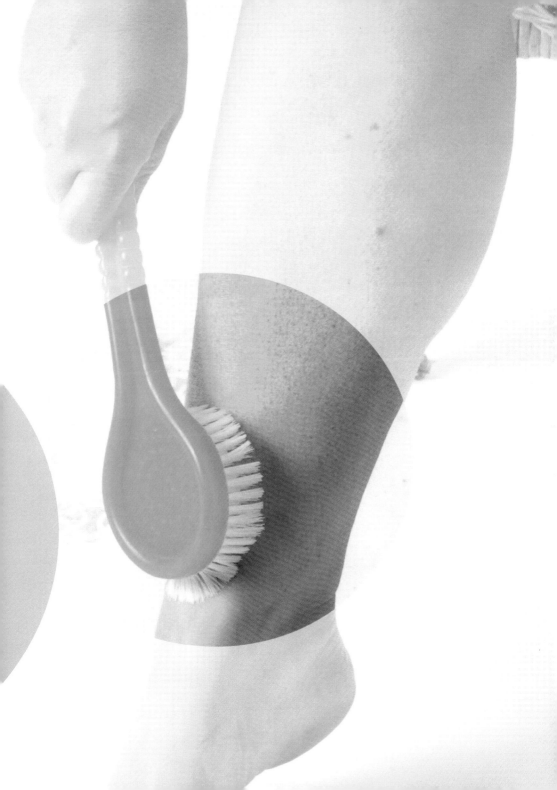

exfoliating

Dry brushing is quick and convenient because it doesn't require anything more than a few minutes each morning and a dry brush. Exfoliation once a week is a great way of removing dead skin cells and for softening areas of hard skin – such as around your heels or elbows – and is a real treat for the body and mind, so make it part of your routine and take the opportunity to indulge yourself. Exfoliating is not harsh – in fact it is very gentle, and can be used on the face and any bits of your body that you find uncomfortable to dry brush, such as around the abdomen.

Unlike dry brushing, exfoliation requires water along with an exfoliating gel or cream. You can buy these – there is a huge range of products in an enormous range of scents – but you can also make your own quite easily. Not only can you save money, but you will have absolute control over what you place on your skin. Since the ingredients of 'home-made' preparations are natural products such as herbs, a little olive oil perhaps and a drop or two of essential oils to perfume, your skin is less likely to experience any adverse reactions.

However, it is worth remembering that if you react to, or are allergic to, a particular foodstuff – strawberries for example – then you are also likely to react to them if you place them on your skin.

Note too that essential oils should not be used if you think you are pregnant – you should not be detoxing anyway – or are trying to conceive, unless they have been prescribed by a fully trained and qualified aromatherapist. Essential oils should not be taken internally and should always be used under supervision, or by following the instructions provided with the oils. Don't just chose an oil because it smells nice: each oil is a drug and each has its own special properties that have effects on both the mind and spirit. And, in common with all other drugs, there may be side effects or contraindications which you must be aware of before using them.

exfoliating scrub recipe

This is so simple to make and easy to use. The exfoliating granules are, in fact, flakes of salt. You can buy coarse sea salt easily in supermarkets – but remember that you won't be eating it on your detox! And if you don't want to spend the extra, you can use ordinary table salt. This is equally effective, and, if you have sensitive skin, you'll find it a little less 'rough' or abrasive. You can use this exfoliating scrub on your face and neck as well, but 'massage' the scrub gently using just one finger in small circular movements and taking care not to drag your skin.

you will need:

Bowl (not metal – a plastic one is best especially for use in the bathroom!)

1 tablespoon of salt – the exfoliant

2 tablespoons of oil – this can be either olive oil, or a vegetable or seed oil such as sunflower oil or grape seed oil

1 tablespoon of honey (set 'thick' honey is preferable but 'runny' honey will work too.) The oil and the honey act as moisturisers on the skin.

Optional: 1–2 drops of essential oil of either fennel or peppermint – either will stimulate your digestion and assist in the detox process.

method:

Mix all the ingredients together to a paste in the bowl!

application:

Run yourself a lovely warm bath, get in and relax for 10 minutes to allow your skin to soften. You can remain in the bath, lift each limb out of the water, and apply a small dollop of the exfoliating scrub in firm but gentle circular strokes all over. Take extra care around your feet, elbows and knees, as this is often where hard skin is to be found! Then put your raised limb back into the bath water and continue with the circular movements until the 'scrub' is washed away, taking all those dead cells with it! If you prefer, you can get out of the bath completely and apply the scrub and then get back in again. When you are finished, towel yourself dry, and apply a body lotion to moisturise and pamper your skin.

bathing

the cold splash

A cold shower? 'No way!' I can hear you say! Well just think about it:

we're encouraged, after cleansing our faces at the end of each day, to

splash with cold water to tone and tighten the skin, so why not the rest

of our body?

When we go on holiday we don't think twice about taking a morning swim in the sea, a lake or even a swimming pool. In fact, we know that it's one of the most invigorating experiences of the whole holiday. Well, if you are lucky enough to live right next to the sea – or have instant access to a pool – you probably do this already. Each day, try paddling barefoot in the sea water up to your ankles, just for a couple of minutes or so.

If you don't live next to the coast, then the next best thing – and equally effective – is a cold shower or bath for just 1 single minute. After your 'normal' shower or bath each morning, bite the bullet and turn the water to cold! If you don't have a shower, empty out the old water, run the cold tap and splash your body with cold water, or even pour a couple of jugfuls over you. The cold water wakes up your body and mind and actually leaves you feeling warmer because the cold water has increased your circulation. It's a terrific way of firming up the skin and improving muscle tone – especially for boobs and bottoms! A cold splash every day keeps 'sagging' away!

epsom salts bathing

While the cold bursts of the shower will wake you up in the morning,
here's a great way to wind down at night. Epsom Salts, which are
inexpensive and easily available at your local pharmacist, are pure
magnesium crystals. Magnesium is vital for the body's cellular activity,
and while the Epsom Salts are for external use only, some can be
absorbed into the body via the skin when the salts are used for bathing.
Furthermore, the salts also speed up the circulation and draw out toxins
from the body – so be prepared to 'glow' for quite a while!

Do not take Epsom Salts internally. Do not take an Epsom Salt bath if you suffer from any skin condition or if you have any cuts and grazes.

Have an Epsom Salt bath once a week only, and it is best to bath in the evening, because you will feel quite warm, relaxed and tired afterwards. Plan your Epsom Salt Bathing session in advance so you'll enjoy it and the great sleep afterwards without interruption.

You will need:

about 1 kg (2 lb) of Epsom Salts – it sounds a lot but the high concentration of salts makes it most effective – and a loofah or massage mitt.

method:

run a deep bath – not too hot – but a comfortable temperature and warm enough to sit in for about 10 minutes without cooling down too much. Pour in the Epsom Salts and stir them around the bath until they have all dissolved.

get into the bath and relax for 5 minutes or so, just to soften up your skin, and then, using your loofah or massage mitt, start massaging your body using gentle strokes and always along your limbs towards your heart. You can gradually increase the pressure of the strokes, and you will notice that you will start to feel warmer. This is the magnesium 'kicking in' – when you start to feel warm, it's time to slow down the massage, so lie back and relax.

when you're through – about 10 minutes in all is enough – get out of the bath and towel dry. Now wrap up warm and cosy, sit or lie down for an hour, and relax some more – play a little soft 'night music' if you like – and soon you'll start to feel comfortably snoozy and ready for a lovely, relaxed night's sleep!

further trea

Here are some more very simple treatments and recipes you can use to personalise your own body beauty programme.

Take a good large bunch of fresh parsley – the greener and leafier the better. Chop it up roughly – stalks and leaves – and place it in a bowl. Pour over a kettle full of boiling water, and leave the parsley to steep until the water is completely cool, then strain off the liquid. You can bottle the liquid and keep it in the fridge, then use it as a wonderful skin tonic that's suitable for all skin types.

nents

If you have dry skin, a good moisturising skin tonic can easily be made by mixing 250 ml (8 fl oz) of rose water– available from pharmacists – and 1 tablespoon of runny honey. Alternatively, enjoy the flavour of an avocado, rub the inside of the skin over your neck and face, then rinse off with tepid water and pat dry. Moisten the skin and close open pores with the very lightly beaten white of an egg. Apply to the skin with fingertips – or a pastry brush!

A facial steam is a great way to thoroughly deep cleanse: the heat makes you perspire, aiding the elimination process and stimulating the circulation. The steam softens the skin, opens the pores and allows the therapeutic benefits of the herbs to be absorbed. For detoxing, try fennel, lime blossom, rosemary or nettles to remove impurities, and boost circulation. You can use two good handfuls of the fresh herb, or about 45 ml (3 tablespoons) of dried herb. Place your selected herb in a good sized bowl and pour over 1½ l (3 pints) of boiling water. Stir briefly – use a clean wooden spoon rather than a metal one – then hold your face over the bowl about 30 cm (12 in) away from the water. Pop a towel over your head and the bowl to make a 'tent', close your eyes – and keep them closed – and stay there for 5–10 minutes. Rinse off with clean water – start with tepid and move on gradually to cool – to close the pores. Then sit down and relax for an hour or so.

scented baths

Depending on the oils or herbs that are added to the water, baths can either be relaxing or invigorating. The easiest way to add 'goodness' to your bath is with a herbal bath bag. You could even hang two or three herbal tea bags from the tap as you fill your bath! A small quantity of herbs – fresh or dried – tied in a square of muslin – or even popped into the toe of an old stocking or tights – and hung from the tap so the warm water flows through and releases the aromatic oils is all you need. It's best to use water that is around blood temperature: too hot and you will perspire in the bath and not absorb any of the herb's properties. Lie back and enjoy the scent for 10 minutes. You will find many of the herbs easily available from health food stores, specialist herbalists, or, you could even grow a few yourself.

therapeutic oil baths

Essential oils must never be used 'neat', directly on the skin. Their properties are highly concentrated and if absorbed into the body can have serious side effects. Instead, all essential oils – and aromatherapy massage oils – must first be diluted in a base or carrier oil, or, dispersed into a medium such as bath water, that will create a suitably dilute solution.

for relaxing baths, choose from: camomile, jasmine, valerian, meadowsweet, lime flowers.

for stimulating baths, choose from: basil, bay, eucalyptus, fennel, ivy, lavender, lemon balm and lemon verbena, mint, pine, rosemary, sage, thyme.

Essential and aromatherapy oils are well known for their beneficial properties. However, it is vital that you select your oil carefully as many do have contraindications: sage, for example, while it clears the skin and firms body tissues, can be quite toxic if not used in moderation. If you are interested in using essential or aromatherapy oils, there are plenty of good, instructional books available, or why not consider enrolling on a recognised course of instruction? The best way to start using essential or aromatherapy oils is to buy 'ready-prepared' blends: this means that they are suitable for 'novice' use and you won't risk making errors in blending or quantities. There are many essential oils available, but some are especially useful in the detoxing process.

Ginger is not only warming and spicy, it's great for digestion. A drop or two of essential oil, or even a good sprinkle of ground ginger in your bath is a great way to keep winter colds away. Half a teaspoon of ground ginger, with a small spoonful of honey to sweeten, and a good squeeze of lemon, all covered with boiling water, makes an excellent digestive and warming tea. Try it after dinner!

Peppermint has long been used to treat digestive disorders but it's also a great pain reliever that is particularly effective for headaches. Invigorating and antiseptic, peppermint oil should be used sparingly – in very low concentrations – especially if you have inflamed or sensitive skin.

Juniper is known to be stimulating, antiseptic and a tonic. It's used to treat aching muscles and skin complaints, including acne and eczema. It's also a diuretic – it makes you expel excess water from your body – and therefore is good for removing waste and toxins. Its stimulating properties – it speeds up the metabolic rate – mean that both your physical and emotional levels are 'lifted'.

Rosemary, as Ophelia in Shakespeare's *Hamlet* reminds us, is 'for remembrance', and how right she was. It's well known as a tonic and is used to stimulate digestion and the circulation: an increase in the flow of oxygenated blood to the brain makes it work better – so your memory seems sharper! Rosemary also encourages hair growth – so steep a sprig of the fresh herb in your rinsing water after you've washed your hair to help keep it full and luxurious.

A very pleasant carrier oil is a tablespoon of almond oil, and it is excellent for dry skin. If you add your essential oil to a carrier oil and then pour this into the bath, you will find you have quite an oily bath, with a fine residue left on your skin. You can massage this into your body afterwards, but, if you do, it's best to have an 'oily' bath at night, so you don't have to dress straight away in 'work clothes' which could be stained.

A less oily bath can be made by simply adding 5–10 drops of your selected essential oil to the bath water when it has settled. Fill the tub first, then sprinkle on the oil and disperse it around and through the water with your hand. Don't add the drops to running hot water: you'll just evaporate them! For an even more 'dispersible' solution, add the drops of essential oil to a tablespoon of milk. It worked wonders for Cleopatra!

Check the temperature of your bath water as this will affect you as well: a relaxing bath should be just below blood heat. For a stimulating bath, the water should be below 85 degrees F (29 degrees C). If the water is too cold, the essential oils won't evaporate as easily and give off their enchanting scent, or release their therapeutic properties, and remember that a too hot bath is not only debilitating, it also ages the skin!

essential oils

You don't just have to bathe in essential oils: essential oil burners are the best way of releasing them into the atmosphere. There are two main types of burners: one type comes with a bowl – which is filled with water to which a few drops of oil have been added – and a container for a candle, the heat of which is sufficient to warm up the water in the bowl so the oils are evaporated into the air. The second type is a dry burner, a terracotta ring that sits on top of an electric light bulb. A few drops of oil are placed on the ring, which is then heated by the light bulb. Whichever you choose, oils should not be used where there are children under 6 years old in the house. Pine is refreshing and uplifting – but can also be very strong, which is why it is often used in commercial cleaning products to disguise base chemical odours and to mask others – so don't

overdo the amount of oil you add to your burner. If pine or any other essential oil is too strong – you may start to develop a headache – add a little more water to your burner bowl, or switch off the lamp and let the ring cool.

exercise

There's no doubt about it: exercise is one of the best ways of enhancing

your body's elimination functions. You don't have to go to the gym; you

don't need to pound the pavements, and, you don't need to do more

than 15 minutes of gentle exercise each day – though if you work up to

half an hour, you'll feel and look even better.

just 15 minutes of gentle
exercise each day can:
heighten our sense of wellbeing and
enhance our self-esteem;
enhance creativity and improve our outlook on life;
increase our IQ and improve the memory;
improve concentration and increase
'mental sharpness';
relieve the 'blues' and help battle depression;
release anxiety;
deepen sleep;
lengthen life;
improve posture, and, it is said,
also improve our sexual performance!

The simplest way to increase your daily exercise is to walk: walk a little way to or from work instead of taking the bus; take a short walk in the park at lunchtime or after work. In summer, take a pleasant stroll in the evening with friends – it's a good way to check out any new neighbourhoods you might want to move to, or get ideas for your garden! In winter, wrap up warm and take a brisk walk, then come home to the cosy warmth of your home. Alternatively, buy – or borrow – a bike, or go for a swim!

What you definitely won't be doing is embarking on a new strenuous fitness routine as this will put too much strain on your body. You can however build up your level of activity and improve your overall fitness little by little. When you've finished detoxing and you feel on top of the world, you can take your exercise programme to equally new heights! Exercise is all too often promoted for its 'fat burning' properties, rather than for its health inducing aspects.

While it certainly does help in weight reduction, when exercise is combined with a restricted calorie intakes – so you burn more than you eat and draw on reserves of fat stored in the body – it often leaves the body weakened and tired and the spirit broken because it is difficult to maintain this strict regime. With detoxing, you are feeding and fuelling your body, energising it, in fact, which will give you the strength and energy to exercise beneficially. Instead of thinking of exercise as a 'battle' with your body, think about exercise as 'making peace' with it, so you can nourish and encourage the natural beauty and graceful movement of your body. Here are some reasons to think of exercise as 'making peace' with your body:

A little exercise, taken every day is better than a 2 hour workout once a week: you won't get bored, you won't get tired out, and you won't give up!

Getting started is the hardest part of any exercise regime – no matter how gentle. But if you think how you can 'slot' little bits of exercise into your daily routine, you'll find it a lot easier. Here are some ideas to get you 'up and at it':

get up and boogie – don't go to the pub – you won't be drinking anyway – go to a club and dance!

walk up and down stairs instead of taking lifts and escalators.

if you are standing in a queue, or at the bus stop – or even sitting at your desk or in front of the TV in the evening – clench and relax your buttocks 10 times! Squeeze in your stomach and then release 10 times or try just sitting and raising each leg in turn.

get your skipping rope out and go for it! Or try out the rebounder and bounce your way to fitness!

put on some funky music and dance and even make dusting and vacuuming part of the routine.

To help you further on your way, try out some of these easy to follow, step by step exercises. You can do them in your own home – or get together with friends and make your own work out session. Try each one and don't overdo it – it's not a race and you are not punishing or battling with your body. Instead, let it stretch and bend naturally, and each time you do the exercises you'll find you can do just that little bit more.

cloches

I call these 'cloches' because you do look a bit like a ringing bell – and that's the action you are aiming for. Lift your right arm and right leg out to the side – not too high to begin with – and then bring both back to the 'centre', immediately lifting your left arm and leg. It's as though you are knocking one leg away and replacing it with the other. How high you lift your leg is not really important and you don't have to keep them too straight either: more useful is to build up a little speed. You'll be quite surprised at how quickly you get hot and sweaty and you will find that this exercise improves your balance and increases the speed of your reactions.

spot walking

This is a very good way of warming up and gently working out the legs. Keep one foot in contact on the floor at all times and gently work through your feet. Don't rush – in fact do this exercise very slowly and you'll feel the warmth run through your feet, ankles and calves.

gentle jog

You don't need to run outside to do this exercise – indoors is fine, but if you have a garden, you could fill your lungs with fresh air at the same time. Once you are warmed up, lift up your knees – you don't have to go too high to start with, just as comfortably as you want. When you've done 10 lifts of your knees at the front, try spot jogging with your heels lifted – as though you are trying to kick your own bottom. Do 10 of these as well. You can increase the number of alternate cycles as you start to feel stronger.

twists

Stand comfortably with your feet shoulder width apart and with your knees slightly bent – this will protect the tendons in the legs and the ligaments around the knees from being twisted and damaged. Stretch your arms out in front of you, clasp your hands, and keeping your arms stretched, twist from your waist to the left and right. Let your head follow the movement of your upper body. Twist slowly and keep the stretch in your arms, and you'll find that before long you'll have increased the distance of your twist – and possibly lost an inch from your waist measurement!

head and neck stretch

This is a very simple exercise and is great for making your neck feel long and lithe. You can do this sitting down or standing, but try to 'lift' your neck – do this by dropping your shoulders (try lifting your shoulders to your ears then letting them drop – that's where your shoulders should be!). Don't tense your neck, keep it 'soft' and keep your chin level – not too high and not tucked in against your chest either! Slowly turn your head to the left, so you are looking over your left shoulder. Focus your eyes on a point – either real or imaginary – on the horizon, and slowly turn your head back to the 'middle' in front of you, and then gently to the right side. Do this slowly and gently 4 or 5 times to each side and notice how each time it is easier to turn your head a little further over your shoulder. Don't 'flick' your head – you'll disturb the fluids in your middle ear which will make you feel seasick!

shoulder stretch

Tension and stress are often most visible – and most uncomfortable – around the shoulders. This simple but effective shoulder stretch works along the top of the shoulder joint and gives that lovely feeling between your shoulder blades as they get 'squeezed' together a little. It's also good for 'opening' the chest – it makes you lift up your bosom in the most regal manner! Stand facing a wall and raise your right arm. Place your palm against the wall directly in front of you – not too high and not too low, just straight out in front. Leaving your hand on the wall, turn your whole body away as far as you can. Return to face the wall and repeat with your other arm.

chair stretch

This is a great way to stretch the bottom and your chest. You'll need a sturdy chair to work with. This is a slow exercise – you're not pumping up and down like a piston but gently lowering yourself, transferring some of your body weight from your legs to your arms as you do so. Place your hands comfortably on the back of a chair, shuffle your body forwards a little so you are a little distance from the chair itself, and gently and slowly bend your knees and lower your body. Feel how your upper chest is being opened and stretched. Using the muscles in your bottom and thighs, push yourself upwards to standing. (Don't pull yourself up with your arms – they need to recover from the stretch!)

back swing

Any exercise that involves kneeling must be approached with extreme care. The knees are easy to injure and difficult to repair, so always make sure that your knees are protected: use a pillow or a large, rolled up towel to kneel on. Never be tempted to kneel directly on the floor – no matter how fluffy your carpet is! Kneel on a pillow, and slowly 'walk' your hands forwards in front of you. When you've reached a comfortable distance, push your bottom backwards towards your heels but leaving your hands in position. Your lower back will arch upwards a little. Next gently swing forwards towards your hands – you will find that your lower back 'drops' into a U-shaped curve here. The arching and dropping of your lower back will help keep it flexible and mobile.

If you find this exercise difficult, try this version instead: stand with your feet shoulder-width apart and knees slightly bent. As if you were doing a sexy 'bump and grind' dance, slowly stick out your bottom, bring it slowly back 'under you' and then slowly thrust your pelvis forwards. You could even go from side to side or 'circle' around. It's surprising how good this feels – it's a very natural movement – but one that our culture doesn't encourage because it is deemed far too sexual! Try it yourself and see!

Once you have become comfortable with these exercises, you can increase the amount of time you spend doing them: build up slowly and gradually if you're not used to exercising and use them to 'warm up' your muscles if you start to introduce more strenuous exercises into your personal detox programme. In the next section, you will find some more suggestions that are not only good for your body, but are also good for the mind and spirit. Remember, detoxing is not about punishing your whole body – and that includes your 'spirit' or 'mind' – it's about valuing, cherishing and nourishing it so it looks, works and feels 'happy' and healthy.

chapter 5

your
detox
programme

your detox pr

Now you've got an idea of the elements of detoxing – the foods you will

be eating, the beauty routine, the energising exercises and the mind and

body balancing, you can begin your programme.

gramme

try and incorporate
your detox into your
normal life – it will
be more fun if
others can join in.

You will need to decide when is the best time for you to start: check your diary and see what events are coming up, how much your workload will be and, if you have a family to shop, cook and care for, how you can integrate detoxing into your daily life. As you will have read, the exercises and the beauty routines don't really take very long – a few minutes extra each day for yourself, and, because all the food is good, nutritious and delicious, there's no reason why you can't serve this for your family – and for your dinner guests as well. Take a look back again at the food lists just to remind you exactly how few things you will be avoiding and how many things are there to be enjoyed in their place. You will find some interesting and inspiring recipes later to try out. For now, you need to decide on the length of your detox programme.

The optimum length of a detox is 30 days. This may seem like a long time, but with a little foresight and planning, you can achieve a great deal. Don't forget the fact that you will be eliminating all the toxins and all the 'bad habits' that you have accumulated over the past years of your life. The slower and gentler the detox, the sooner your body will become adjusted to the subtle changes and you will be giving it time to go through all the cleansing processes – with a little extra help from your new routine. A 30 day detox is really the only way you will achieve a complete detox, so it's worthwhile considering doing it fully and gently. There are, however, shorter length detoxes: you could spend a weekend, a week, or two weeks, the choice is yours. A 48 hour detox will give your body a real break, it will let you see just how good you feel, and it may inspire you to try a 30 day detox the next time around.

Don't be misled by the idea that a 'short' detox of say a week or 10 days means it is a 'short cut': this is quite a sustained period of 'diet' – foods, exercise and body treatments – which instead of being 'spread out' are, in fact, quite compressed.Consequently, you may find the 'effects' more intense and severe. Be completely honest with yourself before you start any detox programme: if you eat junk, drink, smoke, and never take any exercise, then a 10 day detox is going to be a real shock on your body. It would be better to follow a gentler detox over a longer period to allow yourself the time to adjust to the changes and follow up with a maintenance programme to keep you feeling as good as new. If you have already taken steps to improve your health – you are careful about what you eat and you take regular exercise – then a shorter detox, followed by careful maintenance of your good practice and habits will be of benefit.

you drink, smoke and
ke no exercise, you
ally need to follow a
nger detox programme,
avoid 'shocking' your
dy too much.

Whether you opt for a short or longer detox, these are the things you must do each day:

drink a large cup or glass of hot water with lemon juice first thing each morning. It will refresh and revitalise you, cleanse your palate and help flush out all those toxins from your liver. Use filtered water, or bottled, and make sure it has come to the boil, but let it cool a little before you add the lemon juice. In winter to spice it up and warm you up as well, add a pinch of ground ginger.

drink at least 1.5 litres (3 pints) of water during the day. Your morning lemon water will have started you off, but the balance will flush your body – and stop you reaching for tea and coffee. You can, however, enjoy herbal and fruit teas.

eat a minimum of three meals each day, made up of the foods on the recommended foods list (page 156). You should have at least one portion of brown rice every day, and at least three portions of vegetables – one of which should be raw. Don't forget that you can juice your veggies into delicious drinks, or heat up the juice to make thick and creamy soups, lightly stir-fry, steam and bake your vegetables.

eat three portions of fruit and three portions of salad each day. One apple is a portion, one pear is a portion and so on. Again, juicing fruits means that you can enjoy all their goodness in a glass – and you'll end up having significantly more than just three portions! Don't keep your fruit in the fridge, room temperature is better: not only are they not so 'cold' on your digestive system, the flavours will be more intense.

have at least one portion of non-dairy (sheep's, goat's, or soya milk) yoghurt, cheese or milk every day. The nutritional values of these are nearly identical to that of cow's milk products, but are much easier to digest. And great news – this also means that practically any recipe that contains milk, cheese or yoghurt can be adapted to suit your detox programme! So be imaginative when you plan your meals.

eat two portions of either: oily fish – tuna, sardines, mackerel, and herrings; or pulses – beans, chickpeas, millet, quinoa; or nuts (raw, unsalted and fresh, but not peanuts).

don't use more than 1–2 tablespoons of olive oil, nut or seed oil each day.

have one tablespoon of ground flaxseeds every day: you can sprinkle them on your vegetable juices, add them to soups, or sprinkle the whole seeds onto salads.

remember you CAN snack between meals: so prepare some goodie bags of raw carrot sticks, celery sticks, or mixed nuts and seeds – pumpkin, sunflower, sesame seeds. Try some rice cakes and perhaps a little home-made hummus (see recipe page 247).

remember that you are not restricting portion sizes: if you have a salad, make it a good one! If you have a portion of rice, it's a good portion, not something served in some doll's house restaurant! You should feel 'satisfied' with the quantities, quality, and variety of the foods you will be eating.

11 don't eat anything on the **recommended** foods lists if a) you know you are allergic to them or b) you don't like them. Detoxing is not punishment: if you hate the taste of one food, don't torture yourself, simply select an alternative. Enjoying what you eat is good for the mind and the body.

take at least 15 minutes relaxation time each day.

take a cold shower or splash yourself with cold water every morning: don't 'trickle' cold water over you – that's water torture and it'll feel absolutely freezing! Really go for it!

do a self massage every day: you can concentrate on your hands and feet, or follow the sequence described and treat your whole body. It only takes a few minutes.

12 dry brush your skin every morning.

do at least 30 minutes of exercise each day:
start by gently warming up your body with
some of the simple exercises in earlier
chapters, then try the joint opening and
ground exercises, the chi ball, or the yoga
'Salute the Sun'. Don't forget you don't have
to do a 30 minute stint. Increase your amount
of exercise with a pleasant stroll or go for a
swim – you don't have to swim lengths, just
hanging on to the side of the pool and kicking
your legs is wonderful exercise.

17

have 5
minutes doing
your deep
breathing every
day.

every
five days:
take an
epsom salt
bath.

keep your Detox Journal every day: this is
important as you can jot down not only your
physical feelings – your energy levels, the
condition of your skin or hair and so on – but
your emotions and feelings as well. It's OK to
feel low on some days: write this down so
you can check back to see when this
happens – if it's a regular occurrence, or if
it's triggered by particular events or foods.
Write down the good, positive events as well:
what you have achieved, what made you
smile, what made you feel good.

say your
affirmations
10 times
throughout
the day.

looking at these 'must do's' should make you think 'hey, that's easy' and you are absolutely right! It is easy: you may balk a little at the cold shower bit, but everything about detoxing can be fitted into your daily routine. However, you could also take a couple of well deserved days off and spend them just on you, pampering and nourishing yourself.

whenever you can, treat yourself to a professional body therapy: a massage, aromatherapy, reflexology, a manicure or pedicure, or a hair treatment – whatever you want, you deserve it. Check out your local sports centres and health centres for a sauna or Turkish bath treatment.

every

three days:

exfoliate.

devise your programme length:

Whatever length of detox you choose, get yourself a large sheet of paper and draw out a calendar. This is a vital part of the programme, because if you have a concrete plan, written down and easy to see and follow, you are more likely to put all your good intentions into practice.

Now, block in your daily detox routine, plan your menus, and, make sure that you don't miss any of those exciting social engagements at the same time. Add to the calendar your daily list of your 'must do's' – including your exercises and affirmations. Each day, as and when you have completed your 'must do's', tick them off your list and feel a real sense of achievement.

maintaining good habits:

Whether you detox for a weekend or go the whole nine yards and spend a luxurious 30 days transforming your old body into a new, super fit, healthy and relaxed one, what you do afterwards – after you have 'come off' your detox programme – is important too. Over the period you have been cleansing and improving your body, you have also been giving it high quality nourishment, rich in vitamins and minerals. You will also have spent a little more time looking after your skin, hair, and your smile.

start feeling good about yourself and you'll find yourself smiling a lot more!

You will find that your tastes have changed over the course of your detox: not only will you have cleansed your digestive system, but you will have cleansed your palate too, allowing it to savour the true flavours of what you eat. Don't be surprised if you find things taste more intense – you'll certainly notice how processed foods taste hyper-sweet or highly salted – and you'll think how ridiculous it is that the natural flavours are masked by additives and that colourings have to be added to make them look 'real'.

once 'cleansed' you'll start to notice colours, tastes and textures seem more intense.

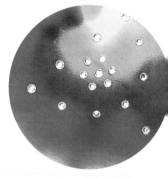

Your sense of smell too, will be heightened: you'll be able to pick out the aroma of individual herbs and spices in a dish, and you may find also that your favourite perfume smells stronger or even different on you! With fewer toxins to handle, your body won't be excreting as many through your skin so your perfume may react a little differently with the natural oils on your skin. That's no problem, there are plenty of perfumes to choose from, so treat yourself!

You'll also be amazed just how intense colours can be – and how subtle they are as well. You'll be quite picky about the foods you want to eat, so you'll be spending a little time looking at them more closely – marvelling at their colours, and arranging menus that look like a still life painting by an old master; smelling the sweetness of fresh produce; hearing their crispness and experiencing their textures as you bite into them.

Your body will have become used to all these new experiences and sensations, all this good, 'self indulgence', so, if when you finish your detox you go off and celebrate with a huge binge of junk food and booze – your body is going to go into shock! The longer and more gentle the detox, the more likely you are to 'wean' yourself off bad habits – and the troublesome foods like sugar, white bread and cakes, cookies and red meats – and the longer the beneficial effects of your detox are likely to last.

There may be times when you do eat these, but you should be prepared for the effects: remember that bloated feeling, the headaches, the limp hair, the spots, the cellulite, the broken nails, the rough skin, the constipation, flatulence...? If you do want to reintegrate some of those 'old' foods back into your diet, then, like the detox programme itself, do so slowly and gently. Add just one food at a time, and monitor your reactions to it – both physical – as reflected in your body and its energy levels – and mental, such as any mood swings or fatigue. If you think that you are having an adverse reaction to that food, you can decide to eliminate it. Think carefully: is that cookie or bar of chocolate really worth the side effects you are experiencing?

By the time you finish your detox you will have developed some very good habits – habits that you can easily continue:

maintain your fluid levels with water.

keep up your exercise and beauty routines.

avoid processed and highly refined foods.

keep off the caffeine.

Think about what you eat: for your body to
work efficiently it needs fuel, and that fuel
should be the best fuel you can give
it. If you eat in a restaurant, always
remember that you are the
customer who is paying (but
you'll be looking so good
that chances are someone
else will be paying!) and
you have a right to
choose. Ask the waiter or
waitress about the
dishes: if there is
something in one you
don't like or want to eat,
don't have it, or ask for it to
be prepared say, without the
cheese. If there is a starter
that you like the sound of, but
nothing on the main course you
want, then ask for the starter as your
main course instead! Restaurants know
you are the customer and are important to
them: they want you to have a good
experience and to return again, so most will

be more than willing to do something a little special – turn a side salad into a main dish, or turn seasonal vegetable accompaniments into a surprising medley of flavours! That's what chefs do, and most will rise to the opportunity to demonstrate their culinary skills!

If you have 'overdone it' – and we all do that at parties, at family get togethers, or when your hosts have slaved away for hours making a fabulous dinner for their guests – you can be safe in the knowledge that once detoxed, you can 'rebalance' your body quite easily by returning to your now regular detox foodstuffs the next day and following it with a 'mini-mini fast' starting at 6 pm and ending the next morning at 8 am.

After your day of detox foods – which are now your everyday foods – at 6 pm eat a very light vegetable/vegetarian supper. That's it! Don't eat anything else until 8 am the next morning – but you can have herbal teas, juices or water in the early evening. At 8 am the following morning, kick start your day – and your liver – with your lemon-and-water hot drink (with a pinch of ginger if you like, or a tiny bit of honey if you must!). Have breakfast, then at lunch, have a meal of fresh fruit, a salad or vegetables. It's not difficult, but it gives your system the time it needs to recover from the 'excesses', won't add any more burden to your system, and provides it with enough fuel to keep it going throughout the day. What could be better?

maintaining good habits doesn't mean you can't enjoy yourself. When you've 'overdone it', try a mini-mini fast to get you back on track.

recipes

Don't for one moment think that detoxing means having to munch your way through a bunch of carrots or a bowl of beans. There are shelves in bookshops and libraries groaning under the weight of thousands of cookery books with recipes from all over the world. Take advantage of all this knowledge – even check out the internet, you'll be amazed at how many recipes you'll find to create a huge variety of dishes that are good enough to entertain royalty! To get you inspired, here are a few suggestions. And don't forget, with a little imagination, you can adapt all your favourite dishes quite easily – just omit the 'no-no's' and substitute with a powerhouse of goodness!

juices

Transforming raw vegetables and fruits into delicious juices means that you can get 500 g (1 lb) of carrots into a big glass! This is a terrific way to get vitamins and minerals in a really concentrated way – and you don't even have to peel them! You can juice just about any vegetable – some are more 'watery' than others – but juicing removes the fibre from fruits and vegetables so they cannot provide the complete nutritional needs of the body: you must have a balance of fats, carbohydrates and proteins to function perfectly. Therefore, try to drink equal amounts of fruit and vegetables juices to avoid consuming too much sugar, which is found in all fruits in the form of fructose.

With a little practice, you'll be able to juice up the most delicious mixes, adjusting the flavours here and there until you have your perfect blend. Remember, too, that as your body becomes more cleansed and efficient, you'll soon notice how juicing concentrates the flavour of each vegetable or fruit, and you will respond to flavours in a much more intense way, so be prepared to adjust the proportions as you detox. By adding some goat's or sheep's milk yoghurt to the fruit juices you can make delicious smoothies – or try goat/sheep milk ice cream in summer for a delicious sundae.

juicing tips:

In hot weather, use frozen berries,
straight from the freezer to chill your drink
– and make an attractive garnish.

Dark green vegetable juices – such as spinach or broccoli – or
dark red veggies – such as beetroot – are not only strong flavours, but acquired
ones too. Ideally, they should be diluted: 4 parts mixer juice to one part dark green or
dark red juice is best. Try carrot or apple juice as the 'mixer' as well as cucumber.
Carrots and apples can be mixed with anything – another fruit or any vegetable.
Generally, vegetable juices should be mixed with other vegetable juices: mix them
with fruit and you'll most likely get flatulence!

Don't make huge quantities: fresh fruit and vegetable juices quickly oxidise –
and may go an off putting brown colour! Keep any leftovers in the fridge.

Do experiment with flavours and combinations: that way you'll
be able to make suitable drinks for breakfast time,
lunch and evenings.

carrot, apple and ginger juice

3–4 large carrots – washed, and the tops
taken off, but there's no need to peel
them

2 apples

1 small piece of fresh ginger, say ½ inch x
½ inch in size, (or half teaspoon of dry
ground ginger)

Carrots and ginger are well known
antioxidants which make this juice a great
'anti-ageing' elixir! The warming properties of
ginger are good for boosting the circulation;
the carrots clean the digestive system and
detox the liver, while the pectin in the apples
binds with those toxic 'heavy metals' such as
lead and mercury and sweeps them out of
the body. And it tastes good too!

Put everything in the juicer. That's it! Serve
straight away.

cabbage cure

Cabbage is iron-rich and full of trace minerals that help keep your hair shining, while the beta carotene in the carrots will help improve the overall condition of your scalp. No more dandruff!

125 g (4 oz) Savoy Cabbage
3 carrots

watercress, carrot and cucumber

This is a real 'fatigue buster': a slightly 'peppery' mix, full of iron to boost energy levels.

2 carrots
large handful of watercress
half a cucumber

parsley purifier

Carrots are great antioxidants and mixed with parsley – which cleanses the breath – and broccoli, they make a juice super-rich in Vitamins E and C which nourish collagen in the skin. Zinc, found in broccoli and all its cruciferous cousins, will help to protect the skin as well providing panthothenic acid (B5) which helps make energy for the body.

3 carrots
4 broccoli florets
handful of fresh parsley

beetroot booster

2 carrots
half a cucumber
⅓ beetroot, scrubbed and chopped.

broccoli and apple

The sweetness of the apple counterbalances the more savoury spiciness of the broccoli. This is definitely one to try – it restores and refreshes at the same time.

2 apples
4 broccoli florets

power booster

This light, purple coloured 'cocktail' is a great way to wind down the day – or wind it up!

2 apples
100 g (4 oz) white grapes
50 g (2 oz) beetroot, scrubbed and
   chopped into chunks
1 cm (½ in) slice of fresh ginger

mange tout mender

Mange tout are, in fact, legumes and are an excellent source of zinc and other trace elements. The juice is a magnificent bright green – admire it briefly before adding the carrots. This is an excellent tonic if you have split, brittle or broken nails – a sign of zinc deficiency!

some mangetouts
a few carrots

green apple blast

The 'zing' of apples, combined with watercress (rich in iron) and parsley, makes for a refreshing and nourishing drink.

2 apples
125 g (4 oz) watercress
handful of fresh parsley

blackcurrant, lemon and apple

Instead of buying one of the 'over the counter' remedies for colds, try this instead. Not only will it taste much better – it will revive your palate and clear your nose – but it will invigorate you as well. The high concentration of Vitamin C will combat persistent 'bugs', while the blackcurrants are also full to bursting with iron and sulphur.

3 apples

1 lemon

**75 g (2½ oz) fresh, frozen, bottled or
canned (in own juice) blackcurrants**

watermelon and honey tonic

As well as being refreshing, this combination is a great 'cleanser' and, it is rumoured, has aphrodisiac properties as well! If you use a sparkling mineral water as a special treat, it really is the juicing equivalent of champagne!

¼ **watermelon, rinds and pips removed**
2 limes, peeled
clear honey to taste
iced water to taste

grape, apple and blackcurrant

A combination of Vitamins E and C to combat the ageing effects of those nasty free radicals.

150 g (5 oz) grapes
150 g (5 oz) blackcurrants
1 apple

dips and sauces
spicy berber sauce

This unusual spicy sauce or marinade originated with the Berbers, the nomadic people of North Africa. It's delicious on roasted vegetables, baked potatoes, with rice or on grilled fish. The toasted spices clear out your sinuses and allow you to fill your lungs deeply! This recipe will make about 200 ml (7 fl oz).

1 small onion, finely chopped

1 garlic clove, finely chopped

1 hot pepper–– jalapeno or chilli – finely chopped

1 inch piece of fresh ginger, finely chopped

1 teaspoon of coriander seeds

1 teaspoon of cardamom seeds, crushed

2 teaspoons of black peppercorns, cracked

⅛ teaspoon of ground cinnamon

⅛ teaspoon of ground allspice

1 clove

5 tablespoons of paprika

115 ml (4 fl oz) olive oil

juice of 1 lemon

Place the onions, garlic, chilli, ginger and all the spices into a dry frying pan and cook over a medium heat for 1–2 minutes, or until the spices are fragrant and lightly toasted. Combine the toasted spices with the cracked peppercorns, the olive oil and the lemon juice in a blender or food processor and blend to a smooth paste.

hummus (chickpea dip)

This is quick and easy to make and you can relish the thought that chickpeas are one of the richest sources of those anticancer agents called protease inhibitors. Chickpeas also help lower blood cholesterol. The tahini – sesame seed paste – provides the 'fat' – approximately 90% of which is unsaturated and high in antioxidant Vitamin E. This recipe will serve six, but it also freezes well! Try it spread on rice cakes.

450 g (1 lb) can of chickpeas, drained
8 tablespoons of tahini
juice of 2 lemons
1 clove of garlic, finely chopped
¼ teaspoon ground cumin
chopped parsley to garnish

Put everything except the parsley in a food processor or blender and whiz until the mixture is smooth. Serve either slightly chilled or at room temperature with chopped parsley sprinkled on top.

grilled radicchio with garlic

This makes a delicious appetiser, salad or main vegetable dish. Radicchio – red leafed chicory – is packed full of carotenoids – which make the reddish colour. The garlic and little bit of olive oil are great for the cardiovascular system. This recipe will serve four – it's easy to make, looks and tastes terrific, so put it on your dinner party menu as well!

2 heads of radicchio – each about the size of an orange

1 tablespoon of olive oil

4 cloves of garlic, finely chopped

a drizzle of balsamic vinegar, to taste

pepper, to taste

Preheat the grill. Cut the radicchio heads in half and sprinkle the cut sides of each piece with a little olive oil and ¼ of the finely chopped garlic. Place the radicchio halves under the heat source on the lowest position for 2–3 minutes, or until the top is justly slightly browned. The radicchio should be slightly warmed but still nice and crispy. Drizzle a little balsamic vinegar over each half, season with pepper and serve.

spiced carrot soup

serves 6

6 large carrots, sliced thinly

1.4 l (2 ½ pints) vegetable stock

**⅛ teaspoon each of: ground cumin,
ground coriander, ground cinnamon,
cayenne pepper**

black pepper to taste

Simmer the carrots with 140 ml (¼ pint) of the vegetable
stock until tender. Puree in a blender or food processor. Return to the pan, add the spices, stir
and add remaining stock and simmer for 20 minutes. Season with pepper to taste.

vegetable stock

makes about 1.4 l (2½ pints)

Any recipe that calls for chicken, or other stock can be substituted with vegetable stock – and any vegetables will work. Here's a suggestion to try:

1 medium onion, chopped

2 carrots, peeled and chopped

2 celery stalks – including leaves – chopped

2 parsnips, peeled and chopped

1 small turnip, peeled and chopped

pepper to taste

1.8 l (3 ¼ pints) water

In a large saucepan combine all the ingredients, bring to boil, lower heat and simmer for 1 hour. Don't be surprised at how 'greasy' vegetables are – simply skim off occasionally – or soak off with a piece of kitchen paper. When the veggies are very soft, remove from heat and strain through a fine strainer. Mash the veggies into a puree to extract all the liquid. Discard the mushy pulp. You can store the stock in the fridge, or try freezing it in ice cube trays – they're great for adding flavour to rice during cooking.

butter beans with apple and cinnamon

serves 4–6

This is an inspired combination of flavours popular in North African and southern European dishes. It's also inspired in the way that both beans and apples lower blood cholesterol, and plus the cinnamon, work further to keep blood sugar levels in check. The touch of turmeric also adds anticancer compounds. Try this winning way with beans with rice and maybe a little grilled fish.

1 tablespoon olive oil

1 large onion, chopped

1 large cooking apple, diced

795 g (1 ¾ lb), or two cans, cooked butter beans –

   (keep the cooking or canning liquid)

¼ teaspoon turmeric

½ teaspoon ground allspice

¾ teaspoon cinnamon

Heat the oil in a large saucepan, add the onions and sauté until golden. Add the apple and seasonings and simmer until soft, but not too mushy. Add the beans and a scant 285 ml (½ pint) of the reserved liquid. Simmer for 10 minutes.

grilled salmon

serves 4

Did you know that eating seafood can protect you from bone fractures? Well it can because seafood is one of the best sources of Vitamin D. Eel has the most Vitamin D per 100 g (3 ½ oz) – a whopping 6,400 IUs. However, since eel is an acquired taste, try salmon instead which weighs in at 500 IUs per 100 g.

4 salmon steaks
4 tablespoons lemon juice
4 teaspoons dried sage
pepper to taste

Brush both sides of the steaks with lemon juice. Sprinkle with sage and season with pepper. Grill until opaque and firm. Try rubbing salmon with garlic and dried herbs – thyme, rosemary, basil and parsley, or even the herb perfectly designed to accompany fish, dill.

the lemony 'have your cake – and eat it too' cake made of chickpeas

serves 8

You really won't believe this, but you can bake a cake and eat it too, without using traditional flour or grains. This cake uses chickpeas – yep, chickpeas – and is actually a Mexican recipe baked on festive occasions. It does use sugar, so it's best kept to a treat.

340 g (12 oz) canned chickpeas, drained and rinsed (discard any loose skins)
4 eggs
225 g (8 oz) sugar
½ teaspoon baking powder
juice and grated rind of 1 lemon

Puree the drained beans in a blender or food processor. Add the eggs, sugar, baking powder and lemon rind to the puree. Pulse a couple of times to combine the ingredients. Preheat oven to 180 degrees C/350 degrees F/Gas 4. Lightly grease a 23 cm (9 in) cake tin, and line base with a circle of greaseproof paper. Pour in the mixture. Bake on centre shelf for 45 minutes – or until a skewer poked into centre comes out clean. Cool on wire rack for 15 minutes, remove cake from tin and allow to cool to room temperature. Before serving, squeeze the lemon juice over the cake and let it soak in.

index

useful addresses

The following organisations can help you locate a professional, qualified and registered practitioner in your area):

The British School of Complementary Therapy,
140 Harley Street,
London W1N 1AH.
Tel: 020 7224 2394 or visit the website at www. bsct.co.uk
(Offers a wide range of treatments, training courses, and essential oils.)

Aromatherapy Organisations Council
3 Latymer Close,
Braybrook,
Market Harborough LE16 8LN

Association of Reflexologists
27 Old Gloucester Street,
London WC1 3 XX

British Acupuncture Council
Park House,
206–208 Latimer Road,
London W10 6RE

British Complementary Medicines Association,
9 Soar Lane,
Leicestershire LE3 5DE

Institute for Complementary Medicine
PO Box 194, London SE16 1QZ

British Association of Nutritional Therapists (BANT)
27 Old Gloucester Street,
London WC!N 3 XX
Tel: 0870 606 1284

Institution for Optimum Nutrition (ION),
Blades Court, Deodar Road,
London SW15 2NU
Tel: 020 8877 9993
(Both organisations will provide a list of qualified nutritionists who can arrange tests for food intolerances and yeast sensitivities, and develop personal nutritional eating plans.)

Vegetarian Society
Parkdale,
Dunham Road,
Altrincham, Cheshire WA14 4QG
www.vegsoc.org

Yoga For Health Foundation,
Ickwell Bury, Ickwell Green,
Biggleswade,
Bedfordshire SG18 9EF

stockists of foodstuffs:

Simply Organic Food Company Limited,
Olympic House, 196 The Broadway,
London SW19 1SN
Tel: 0845 1000 444
Fax: 0845 1003 020
www.simplyorganic.net
email: orders@simplyorganic.net
(everything organic, and all delivered to your home or office throughout the UK. Open 24 hours, 7 days a week!)

bibliography

Baker, S.M. (MD) *Detoxification and Healing*, Keats Publishing Inc, 1997

Bennett, P. & Barrie, S. *7-Day Detox Miracle*, prima Health, 1999

Brignell, R. *Beginner's Guide to Pilates*, D&S Books, 2001

Bristow, S. *The Herbal Medicine Chest*, Gramercy, 2002.

Brown, D.W. *Beginner's Guide to Reflexology*, D&S Books, 2000

Carper, J. *The Food Pharmacy*, Simon & Schuster, 1991

Houlahan, F. *The Beginner's Guide to Classic Yoga*, D&S Books, 2001.

Millidge, J. *The Juicing Handbook*, Silverdale Books, 2002.

Pawlett, R. *Beginner's Guide to Tai Chi*, D&S Books, 2000.

Savill, A. & Hamilton, D. *Super Energy Detox*, Thorsons, 2002

Scrivner, J. *Total Detox*, Piatkus, 2000

credits

The author and publishers would like to thank everyone involved in the

production of this book. Special thanks to Caron and Channing for

modelling duties!

Yoga postures p92-99 from

The Beginner's Guide to Classic Yoga,

by Frances Houlahan,

D&S Books Ltd © 2001.

Reflexology sequence p122-9 from

An Introduction to Reflexology

by Denise Whichello Brown,

D&S Books Ltd © 2000.